A History of the English Bible

by
Jonathan Underwood

 STANDARD PUBLISHING

Cincinnati, Ohio   39974

Appreciation and gratitude are expressed to Jonathon R. Stedman for his contribution to the writing of this book. His work can be seen in the introduction and chapters 1, 2, and 5.

Chapter 13, "An Evaluation of Some Current Translations," is adapted from *Selecting a Translation of the Bible,* by Dr. Lewis A. Foster. Copyright 1978, 1983, The STANDARD PUBLISHING Company, Cincinnati, Ohio. Used by permission.

Sharing the thoughts of his own heart, the author may express views that are not entirely consistent with those of the publisher.

Library of Congress Cataloging in Publication Data

Underwood, Jonathan, 1955-
  A history of the English Bible.

  1. Bible. English—Versions—History. 2. Bible—History. 3. Bible—Evidences, authority, etc. I. Title.
BS196.U53 1983   220.5'2   83-577
ISBN 0-87239-644-4

Table of Contents

95226

Introduction

Most Christians, as they read through the pages of the Bible, do so with the understanding that they are reading "the Word of God." However, though they hold unswervingly to the divine origin of the Bible, most readers probably have little knowledge regarding the processes which have occurred in bringing this "Word" from the mind of God to the modern versions of the Bible now available. How could the will of God be "translated," as it were, into the language of men? Who wrote the Bible? God? Men? Or both? Why are there sixty-six books in the Bible, and how did these particular books become the Bible, to the exclusion of others? How did the Hebrew and Greek originals become the King James Version, or any other English translation?

The answers to these and many other questions are available to the student of the Bible. Many volumes have been written on the subjects of the writing, collecting, and translating of the Word of God. The aim of the present study is to examine briefly all three of these areas, in order to obtain a clearer grasp of the processes by which the will of God came to be the Bible we now possess.

1

Revelation

The Necessity of Revelation

The doctrine of revelation must begin with the creation of man. As soon as a creature with the ability to reason existed, God was committed to revealing himself. The first pair of human beings had been placed in a beautiful environment. They were totally innocent, and yet, by virtue of their proximity to a forbidden tree, the man and woman were in imminent danger of forfeiting their innocence. How were they to know? The revelation of the will of God, and ultimately, of God himself, was made absolutely essential by the purpose of God for this creature.

Thus, God had created a being in His own image. Man was made with the ability to communicate, and it is to be expected that this ability would be used. If there is no revelation of God, then the creation of man cannot be accounted for. He is, furthermore, not responsible for whatever fate awaits him, for he has no conception of what is expected of him. The purpose of God for man requires that God reveal himself.

Creation Requires Revelation

Now if God were a man with a visible body, He could simply walk onto the stage and become one of the characters in the drama of world history. But the very nature of God is spiritual (John 4:24). Theologians refer to Him as "transcendent," that is, He exists outside of the world. Because of this aspect of God's nature, if man is to know anything about Him, God must take the initiative to reveal himself. Even with all of the revelation that He has provided, it is impossible to comprehend God's infinite nature.

Imagine the chaotic condition of man's understanding if revelation were not provided!

Both the nature of God and His purpose for man require that revelation be communicated to the creature made in His image. But there is a further step, a much more significant one, necessitating the revelation of God's nature and will: man has sinned, and has marred the image of God in which he was created. Within the heart of every man is that voice known as the conscience, that whisper that tells him that he has done something wrong. Contrary to the pervasive relativism taught by modern philosophy, which holds to the view that there is no absolute moral standard, guilt is still as always a major factor in human society. We *know* we have done wrong. Thus, pagan cultures offer sacrifices to various deities, to turn aside their wrath for sin. More "civilized" people turn to alcohol, suffer severe strains in relationships, and even commit suicide because of a deep sense of guilt for injuries they have inflicted on others. God calls the wrong that all men have done *sin*. And the fact of sin makes it necesary for God to reveal himself.

The inclination in man is to close the lines of communication between himself and God. After demonstrating that both Jew and Gentile are under sin, Paul quoted from the Old Testament: "There is no one righteous, not even one; there is no one who understands, no one who seeks God" (Romans 3:10, 11). It is this fact of unrighteousness that makes it imperative for God to act, if anything is to be done to remedy the situation.

Redemption Requires Revelation

And He has! Immediately following the first transgression, God set in motion a plan that would culminate in the sacrifice of His own Son for the redemption of His creation. The goal of the cross was the salvation of mankind, but in order for it to have any effect, it must be explained. Thousands of people died on crosses, and Jesus would be just a statistic if His redemptive death were not interpreted. Furthermore, the implications of this redemption are so far beyond the comprehension of finite men that the interpreta-

8

tion must be provided by God himself. This interpretation of the salvation-events is called revelation. Without it, there is no redemption.

Therefore, we have seen that revelation is essential for at least three reasons. God's creation of man in His image requires it. The nature of God must be revealed to be perceived. In addition, the fact of sin and the plan of salvation provided for its forgiveness require that the author of the plan should explain it. So revelation of some sort is necessary.

Types of Revelation

If God, recognizing this necessity, had chosen to reveal himself at one time, or by one method, it may have been sufficient. On the other hand, questions could be raised regarding the objectivity, or even the sanity, of the person to whom the revelation came. God did not, however, leave the situation in such a state. "In the past God spoke to our forefathers through the prophets at many times and in various ways" (Hebrews 1:1). We will now look at these "various ways" by which God has revealed His message.

General Revelation. The very creation itself bears witness to the nature of God. The psalmist David exclaimed, "The heavens declare the glory of God; the skies proclaim the work of his hands" (Psalm 19:1). God's kindness is **Creation Reveals God** seen in the weather and in the agricultural cycle (Acts 14:17). Paul states that men are without excuse for their wickedness, "since what may be known about God is plain to them, because God has made it plain to them. For since the creation of the world God's invisible qualities—his eternal power and divine nature—have been clearly seen, being understood from what has been made" (Romans 1:19, 20). Thus, God has revealed himself to *all* men in the creation, and according to Paul, any failure to recognize God is a deliberate suppression of knowledge.

History. God has acted in events in history, and in seeing those events, the participants witnessed the revelation of

God's power. Who could see the Red Sea or the Jordan River parted, and not know that God was acting? God needed to teach Jonah an important lesson; so He intervened dramatically in the prophet's life. Many other events and miracles in both Testaments can be cited as evidence, and the entire history of the Biblical nation of Israel illustrates the activity of God.

Dreams and Visions. Here God reveals a message directly to the mind of the recipient. No event happens external to the dreamer; the revelation is completely in his mind. Examples of these types of mental revelation are seen in the lives of Abram (Genesis 15), Joseph (Matthew 1:20; 2:13, 19), and Peter (Acts 10:9-17).

Oral Revelation. On a few occasions, God actually spoke directly from Heaven. When Moses was on Mount Sinai, the Lord spoke to him in a direct way. In fact, God stated that He conversed with Moses "face to face" (Numbers 12:8). After Jesus' baptism, God spoke from Heaven, identifying Jesus as His Son (Matthew 3:17).

Written Revelation. There were two occasions when God himself provided a revelation written by His **God Himself** own hand. The first was the giving of the **Wrote a Message** Ten Commandments, written on two tablets; "the writing was the writing of God" (Exodus 32:16). In the second instance, God personally delivered a message to the arrogant King Belshazzar, informing him of the demise of his kingdom (Daniel 5:5, 23, 24).

Appearances. God has revealed himself to men by presenting himself in a physical form, and then speaking from this visible presence. These appearances are called "theophanies." God appeared in this manner to Abraham, Hagar, Manoah, and others, often under the title of "the angel of the Lord."

The Incarnation. The climax of God's revelation came when His Son, himself Divine, came to this planet and became a man. Jesus said to Philip, "Anyone who has seen me has seen the Father" (John 14:9). John writes, "No one

10

has ever seen God, but God the only Son, who is at the Father's side, has made him known" (John 1:18). The climactic character of Jesus' revelation of God's message is vividly presented by the writer of Hebrews, when he states that "in the past God spoke to our forefathers through the prophets at many times and in various ways, but in these last days he has spoken to us by his Son" (Hebrews 1:1, 2).

It must be noted here that this is not the only reason Jesus became a man, nor is it the primary reason He came. He told His disciples that He came "to give his life as a ransom for many" (Mark 10:45). In the working out of man's **The Incarnation— the Ultimate Revelation** redemption, however, the Son of God also provided the ultimate disclosure of the character and message of God.

So these are the means by which God has revealed himself to men through the ages. There is, however, one question remaining: how has God given His message to those of us who have not seen a prophet or heard an apostle?

Written Revelation

God created man with the ability to communicate. There are several methods by which communication can take place, but it is normally accomplished by means of words. The transcendent, omniscient Creator of our ability to verbalize our thoughts certainly has the power to speak to us in our own language.

Furthermore, the wisdom of God anticipated the need for a continuing record of His revelation, and He himself commissioned various people to put it in writing. "Then the Lord said to Moses, 'Write down these words' " (Exodus 34:27). Concerning His oracle to His rebellious people, God commanded Isaiah: "Go now, write it on a tablet for them, inscribe it on a scroll, that for the days to come it may be an everlasting witness" (Isaiah 30:8). Similar instructions were given to Jeremiah (Jeremiah 30:2).

In the New Testament, the Gospels are a written record of God's ultimate revelation of himself through His Son. Other portions of the New Testament are also the product

11

of revelation, as Paul makes clear in 1 Corinthians 2:7ff; 4:1; 7:10; 11:23; 15:3. Other passages also attest to the fact of revelation. (The other divine process involved in the writing of Scripture, inspiration, is discussed in the second chapter of this work.)

The debt of gratitude that we owe to God for providing this book is immense. The Bible is often so **Bible's "Indispensable Significance"** taken for granted that its indispensable significance is sometimes forgotten. The great Princeton scholar, Benjamin Breckinridge Warfield (*The Inspiration and Authority of the Bible,* P and R, 1979, pp. 126, 127), summed it up well:

> We may say that without a Bible we might have had Christ and all that he stands for to our souls. Let us not say that this might not have been possible. But neither let us forget that, in point of fact, it is to the Bible that we owe it that we know Christ and are found in him. And may it not be fairly doubted whether you and I,—however it may have been with others,—would have had Christ had there been no Bible? . . . No: whatever might possibly have been had there been no Bible, it is actually to the Bible that you and I owe it that we have a Christ,—a Christ to love, to trust and to follow, a Christ without us the ground of our salvation, a Christ within us the hope of glory.

2

Inspiration

When God communicated His message directly to a human recipient, the possibility of a garbled or incorrect message was eliminated. In the recorded instances of direct revelation in the Bible, the one who received the communication had no difficulty in apprehending the exact words God wished him to know.

A problem is introduced into the process of revelation when the prophet transmits the message to others. Whenever a third party is used in communication, the danger of error is present. This is vividly illustrated by the old party game, "Gossip," in which one person whispers something to another, who relays it to another, and so on around a circle. The final statement often bears no resemblance to the original. With the recipient of direct revelation expected to pass it on in writing to his contemporaries, and with God's foreknowledge that this writing would be passed on to successive generations, the problem of protecting the truth of the message for all time required a further step in the process. This step we call "inspiration."

Inspiration Guards Truth

Under the protection of this process, the writing of the Bible was entrusted to men. These authors were not infallible; they included a man with a serious problem with his temper, an adulterer, a repentant apostate king, an apostle who on one occasion "stood condemned," and a man who considered himself "the worst of sinners." It was, however, their task to put God's Word on paper. While God *could* have delivered the Bible in a different way, eliminating the "middle man," He chose not to. God has always chosen to

13

work with man through a human agency. Thus, with this method established, inspiration becomes necessary to guard the accuracy of the message.

What Is Inspiration?

First, inspiration means that the ultimate responsibility for the contents of the Bible lies with God. It contains what God deemed necessary for man's good. There are many things that we might have wished to be included. Some would like specific answers from God regarding decisions that must be made; others are concerned whether or not a certain activity is a sin; still others would appreciate it if every theological question were answered. God chose, however, to leave us a comparatively small volume, containing His scheme of redemption and principles for living, which in conjunction with the rational capability with which He created us, is sufficient to point us in the right direction.

Second, the doctrine of inspiration recognizes that not everything in the Bible is revelation. This may at first appear to approach heresy, but the Bible itself bears witness to this fact. The author of 2 Chronicles (perhaps Ezra) knew the prophesied length of the Babylonian exile by reading Jeremiah (2 Chronicles 36:21). Joshua quotes from the Book of Jashar (Joshua 10:12, 13). Luke refers to the research he undertook to investigate material for his Gospel (Luke 1:3).

Inspiration Complements Revelation

Personal experience also was a source for material. Much of the material in Acts, for example, did not need to be "revealed" to Luke; he was there when it happened (Acts 16:10—28:16). Revelation was unnecessary where research and experience were possible. So, while much of the Bible had to be revealed because of the nature of the material, not all of it is revelation.

Inspiration, however, applies to all of Scripture. It was necessary to ensure that not only the revealed portion was accurate, but also the portion based on memory and historical research. Ezra wrote of events that happened centuries

14

before his own time. Perhaps his sources were overly harsh or overly gracious to particular kings. Inspiration was God's way of guarding historical accuracy. Perhaps Peter told Luke what he preached about at Pentecost; but that had been thirty years previous, in the midst of the most incredible experience of his life. Inspiration enabled Luke to record the portion of the address that God knew would be valuable for later generations of readers.

Inspiration is the Holy Spirit's influence upon men. Its purpose is to guard the accuracy of the communicated message. A significant question must be raised at this point: how did the Spirit perform this influence? To answer this question requires a brief look at several theories that have been offered in an effort to explain inspiration.

Theories of Inspiration

Mechanical dictation. The view held by many ancient writers was influenced greatly by Plato, who referred to inspiration as "ecstasy." The **Theories Vary** seer was much like a musical instrument, a **Widely** passive instrument in the hands of God. He was possessed, his human faculties suspended. It was a small step, then, for Philo, a Jewish contemporary of Jesus, to explain inspiration as mechanical dictation. He is said to be the model for later Christian ideas on inspiration. This view states that God told Moses, Luke, Peter, and the others exactly what to write in their books and letters. He dictated the material.

Ordinary inspiration. In this view, Paul and Peter were not different in quality from any other Christian writer. A person who possesses a great skill in verbal communication is often said to have been "inspired" when he wrote a certain poem or essay, or when he gave a particular speech. This theory says that this is what the Biblical writers had: a great, but non-supernatural, ability to communicate.

Dynamic inspiration. The writers are said to have been given *general* guidance in terms of the areas or contents to be included, but no specific guidance.

15

Partial inspiration. Matters essential to our salvation and morality are inspired, according to this theory, while non-essential matters are not.

Plenary inspiration. This view holds that all Scripture is inspired, not just part. It is not the same as the dictation theory, however. It merely asserts that God exercised the control and supervision necessary for the human authors to write His Word. At times He may have dictated. At other times, He needed to do almost nothing as the human authors had accurate information already available.

Verbal inspiration. According to this view, every word of Scripture is inspired. It does not suggest that God always chose the exact words the human authors wrote, however. Thus, it is also different from the dictation theory. It does hold, however, to the idea that every word of Scripture is significant, and God insured that the very words chosen by the human authors best conveyed God's will and purpose.

What Scripture Itself Says

Turning from the theories to the Scripture, one is interested to note that the Bible nowhere explains the mode of inspiration. Any attempt to identify the mode must thus proceed inductively. And the process will be affected by one's presuppositions regarding the possibility of divine intervention in the world. If this is denied, then a view ranging from dynamic inspiration to ordinary inspiration will result. If it is accepted to the exclusion of any ordinary human process, then a view of mechanical dictation is sure to result. Verbal and plenary inspiration are possible conclusions only if one assumes the possibility of divine intervention in a human process.

Presuppositions Affect Understanding

We will here accept Scripture's claim to divine intervention. What, beyond this, can we say of inspiration? Close examination of the Scriptures makes it apparent that the method of inspiration varied. Some parts of Scripture clearly were dictated. The prophetic passages that begin with, "Thus saith the Lord," or a similar formula are the very

16

words of God himself (for example, Isaiah 43:1; Jeremiah 2:5; Ezekiel 14:2, 12). The letters to the seven churches in Asia were given to John (Revelation 2:1, 8, 12, 18). These passages are a matter of direct revelation, as discussed earlier. In other cases, however, only general supervision would be necessary to ensure the statements were true. For instance, Paul's greeting to the Roman church in Romans 1:1-15 contains material that need not require that it be dictated; the apostle is here merely saying "hello" to the Christians there. The writers were aware that the Holy Spirit was working in them (see 1 Corinthians 7:40); but the way in which He worked to ensure accuracy was probably subconscious.

Since the method of writing is not described in the Scripture, it seems clear that this is not nearly as important as the result; the process is not as crucial as the product. Peter writes that men "were carried along by the Holy Spirit" (2 Peter 1:21); thus, men can truly be said to be "inspired writers." But the only use of the word "inspired" in the older translations of the Bible is found in 2 Timothy 3:16, and there it is the Scripture that is said to be "inspired." The word there is *theopneustos,* and this word means "God-breathed." We are not told how God inspired it; but we are told that it is inspired. This passage also indicates plenary inspiration: *"All* Scripture is God-breathed."

Scripture Claims Plenary Inspiration

Furthermore, the inspiration of Scripture extends to the words that are written; inspiration is *verbal.* God did not always choose the exact words. If this were the case, how could one explain the great differences in style between, for example, the apostles Paul and Peter? There are even stylistic differences between Paul's earlier epistles and his later ones, written fifteen years apart. No theory of dictation can explain this. But without verbal inspiration, no one can explain Paul's argument on the basis of a single word of Scripture in Galatians 3:16. Thus, the Holy Spirit may have allowed flexibility in the choice of words, but limits would be established beyond which a writer could not go.

17

In any case, the product is the important thing. Although written by many authors with definite styles, the product is inspired of God: it is *His* word. Thus, J. W. McGarvey points out, in *Evidences of Christianity,* that inspiration does not exclude: a.) the individual style and vocabulary of the writers; b.) the expression of the writers' personal feelings; c.) free quotation from the Old Testament; d.) citation from the Septuagint as the Word of God; e.) free interpretation of Old Testament prophecies; f.) variations in the reports of the same events; g.) ignorance on the part of the writers concerning various things not connected with their writing; h.) imperfections in the character of the writers; i.) personal remarks by the writers.

God used human writers to write His book. But He made sure that it was *His* book. This is inspiration.

Infallibility of Scripture

If we accept the plenary and verbal inspiration of Scripture, if we accept Scripture as the Word of God, then we must accept the infallibity of Scripture. Much could be said about this matter, but the issue really centers around the credibility of Jesus himself. The Son of God taught that the Scripture is irreproachable in John 10:35. In addition, He used the Scriptures in His teaching as if they were accurate. He accepted the historicity of Old Testament events and people. He taught that prophecy would be, indeed *must* be, fulfilled (Luke 24:25, 26; Matthew 26:54). When asked what was necessary to inherit eternal life, Jesus referred the inquirer to the law (Luke 10:25, 26); the teaching of the Old Testament was considered normative in ethical matters. In every area, the Lord used the Scripture as the infallible Word of God. The apostle Paul maintained this same attitude, even to the point of basing an important argument on whether a word in Genesis was singular or plural (Galatians 3:16).

Now there are two choices. Either the Gospel records are incorrect, and Jesus never taught the infallibility of the Bible,

Jesus Accepted Infallibility

or the Gospels are correct. If the Gospels are accurate, Jesus is either wrong or is accommodating himself to the incorrect beliefs of His hearers, or He is right about Scripture. If either the Scripture or Jesus can be called in question, then our faith has no foundation upon which to stand.

Furthermore, it seems reasonable to suppose that if God revealed His message to various authors, and if He inspired the product so that it contained what He wished to be included, then the result would be free from error. If the Bible is fallible, it cannot be inspired. If it is inspired, it must be infallible. Its author ultimately is God himself.

We will see in a later chapter that the process of the transmission of the books resulted in several "corruptions" of the text. So it is necessary to add here that the infallibility of the Biblical books applies only to the original copy. In other words, the book of Romans was dictated by Paul to his scribe Tertius, and that original was inspired. Then, as uninspired men began to make copies, and copies of copies, problems crept in. But the original text was the infallible and inspired Word of God.

Original Manuscripts Infallible

Is inspiration important? If our hope rests on the solid rock of Christ, and yet the only place from which we obtain our information about Him is sinking sand, then there is actually little basis upon which to build our hope. Jesus and His apostles taught that the Bible is God's inspired Word. If they were in error here, where can they be believed? The absolutely crucial nature of the inspiration of the Scripture is not just a subject for discussion by learned theologians. It is the basis upon which the simple faith of every Christian rests. "Jesus loves me, this I know; for the *Bible* tells me so."

3

The Authority of the Bible

Sports World magazine has been called the sports "bible." Other books and magazines have
Bible Implies Authority also been called "bibles" in their respective fields. Why? Authority. The authority of the Bible is recognized so much that the term *bible* itself has become a metaphor for authority. Dictionaries recognize this, giving as a definition of *bible* "a publication that is preeminent esp. in authoritativeness" (*Webster's New Collegiate Dictionary,* 1981, p. 106).

So the question is not whether, but what. What is the nature of the Bible's authority? That is, how and why is it authoritative? And for all the recognition that the Bible has authority, this question remains hotly debated.

The authority of the Bible is based on the revelation and inspiration of the Bible. If the Bible has God as its ultimate source, then its authority also has God as its source. Traditionally, this has been the orthodox position on Biblical authority. Since "all Scripture is inspired by God" (2 Timothy 3:16), then the whole Bible enjoys divine authority.

The Purpose of the Bible

The authority of the Bible must be considered in the context of the purpose of the Bible. Man is in need of God's revelation for redemption. Jesus came "to seek and to save the lost," and it is the Bible that provides man with information regarding the redemptive work of Christ.

20

The purpose of the Bible, then, is primarily to provide an authoritative answer to the question, "What must I do to be saved?" It is not the purpose of the Bible to provide textbook accounts of history, science, or geography. Thus, the **Not a Textbook** Bible ought not to be used extensively for such purposes, for its information is incomplete. What it does give complete information on are matters of "teaching," "reproof," "correction," and "training in righteousness; that the man of God may be adequate, equipped for every good work" (2 Timothy 3:16, 17, *New American Standard Bible*).

Only God is able to forgive sin (Mark 2:7); thus, only God's Word carries the authority for the question of salvation. And it has provided the answer to man's predicament for centuries. Unfortunately, it has also been used as authority in areas in which it does not provide *complete information*. Galileo was persecuted for denying the Bible when he wrote that the sun, not the earth, was the center of the solar system.

However, to say the Bible gives *incomplete* information is not to say it gives *false* information. Galileo did not deny the Bible or its authority, for the Bible says nothing about the center of the solar system. Modern science has yet to contradict anything the Bible actually says, though it has, at times, refined our thinking about creation.

Different Views of the Bible's Authority

Today there are many different views of the Bible's authority. Each position is considered divisive by those who hold other views. Apparently, division is not the real issue, but an attack on the integrity of persons who hold particular views. It is better to consider the positions themselves than to slander the persons behind them.

The Authority of Scriptural Silence. This view holds that not only is everything the Bible says authoritative, but so is what the Bible does not say. Arguing from silence is valid under this system, for whatever the Bible does not allow is considered sin. Following this principle, certain sects have

21

drawn apart from society, rejecting modern technology. It is a difficult position to hold, however, as is obvious from the diversity among such groups as to how much or how little they will allow.

The Authority of Scriptural Fact. This view holds that everything the Scriptures affirm as factual is authoritative, but only what they affirm. **Where Scripture Speaks, We Speak. . . .** Thus, where Scripture is silent, the Christian is free to choose whether or not he will participate in a given activity. What Scripture commands, he is bound to obey. What Scripture forbids, he is bound to avoid. Beyond that, he is at liberty.

There are more facts recorded in Scripture, however, than those which command or prohibit moral behavior. Although it is not the purpose of Scripture to provide a textbook account of history, geography, or science, certain facts from those fields must necessarily be recorded. Twelve Old Testament books, as well as Acts in the New Testament, are called "history." Beyond that, several other books, including the Gospels and many of the prophets, also contain historical narratives. Under this view of Scriptural authority, these accounts are held to be assuredly true. The book of Acts has been repeatedly attacked as a historical document. Still, no scholar has ever been able to prove that Luke made any mistakes. Acts is historically reliable.

The Authority of Scriptural Teaching. This view differs from the last in that it seeks to recognize that Scripture is not intended to be the final word in matters not related to salvation and ethics. Only what the Bible *teaches* is authoritative in this view. Whatever else the Bible affirms in the course of its teaching may or may not be true. Those who hold this view do not deny the inspiration of Scripture. In fact, many have signed their names to documents affirming inspiration. But their view of inspiration holds that God inspired only the moral teaching of the Bible, and not the history, geography, and science.

The Absence of Scriptural Authority. This view of authority has some variations, but its basic premise is to deny inspiration. Some would hold that only the words attributed directly to God or Jesus are authoritative, the rest being men's opinions. Others would hold that even the quotations of God and Jesus are but men's impressions of divine thought and are, therefore, not authoritative. These would like to be their own authority, and resist the authority of Scripture in order to set their own moral codes and concepts of grace.

The Traditional View. The traditional view of the authority of Scripture is what has here been called the authority of Scriptural fact. From the beginning, Scripture was recognized as being absolutely true and authoritative in all it affirmed. Problems arose when men attempted to give to their own assumptions this same authority, but the solution is not to deny Scriptural authority to Scripture. The solution is to recognize precisely what the Bible does and does not say.

This was the problem in Jesus' day. The Jews recognized the absolute authority of Scripture. The scribes and Pharisees, however, had elevated their traditions to the same level of authority. It was not with Scripture that Jesus clashed. He fulfilled Scripture. But it was tradition that Jesus confronted and challenged.

Tradition's Authority Challenged

Luther clashed with the same kind of authoritative tradition in the sixteenth century. He stood firmly on the authority of Scripture. The Roman Catholic church opposed him with the authority of tradition and of the pope. The Catholic church continues to add the authority of tradition to the authority of Scriptures: "Holy Mother Church has always believed and believes that the full revelation is contained not in Scripture alone but in Scripture and Tradition, as in two sources, though in different ways" (Avery Dulles, S.J., "The Authority of Scripture: a Catholic Perspective," Frederick E. Greenspahn, ed., *Scripture in the Jewish and Christian Traditions: Authority, Interpretation, Relevance,* Nashville: Abingdon, 1982, p. 33). The rest of the Christian world has limited authority to Scripture alone.

It is a departure, then, from the traditional view to hold

that parts of Scripture are not authoritative. This is not to say, in and of itself, that the view is wrong. Many, however, seem to fear that a rejection of the traditional is a rejection of orthodoxy; so they deny that their view is different from the traditional view. But those who would hold this relatively new concept must recognize that they are breaking with tradition.

Inerrancy

Is the whole Bible authoritative? The traditional view, that it is, is generally called *inerrancy*. This con-
Scripture's cept is committed to the reliability of God as
Authority Upheld the ultimate author of Scripture. Since it is impossible for God to lie or be deceived, then nothing that the Bible affirms, even incidentally, can be in error. This includes history, science, and geography.

The Bible itself claims inspiration for its entirety in 2 Timothy 3:16. Thus, the whole Bible, not just certain parts, must be recognized as having God as its author. Nothing the Bible says is in error.

The history of the Bible may serve to illustrate the point. The Bible was not written solely for twentieth-century readers. It was written for people contemporary with the events recorded. Any inaccuracies in the history recorded could thus be refuted. But Scripture was accepted immediately as authoritative, for no errors were found. The Gospel writers, then, did not make up historical settings or put words into the mouths of Jesus and His contemporaries to demonstrate their own understanding of Jesus. The events really took place. Jesus really did perform miracles, He really did cleanse the temple (twice), and He really did enter Jerusalem while the crowds hailed Him as the Messiah. If He hadn't, there would be many who would have refuted the Gospels as false, and the moral truth contained in the historical fiction would have been lost.

Interpretation

There is one major problem in the concept of Scriptural

authority. That problem is interpretation. Just what does the Bible say? What is the answer to the question, "What must I do to be saved?" Many people, reading the same Bible, offer several answers. Many other questions meet a similar fate.

More division is caused in the church by this problem than by the problem of how much of the Bible is authoritative. In this issue, two sides **Division Caused** draw apart, both claiming the full authority **by Faulty** of Scripture to be behind them. **Interpretation**

Proof texts. It has been said that a person can use the Bible to prove anything. The charge is probably correct. Certain portions of Scripture can be removed from context, joined with other verses also out of context, and made to say just about anything. Certainly some very different and downright opposite conclusions can be drawn. The problem is not with Scripture, but in interpretation. Scripture must be taken in context to be properly understood. Lifting verses out of context may support an opinion, but it does not provide "a word from the Lord."

Reading into a passage. This is similar to the problem of proof texts in that the interpreter again has a preconceived notion that he is attempting to support. Thus, he sees more in a passage than is there. He distorts the context by injecting twentieth-century meanings on first-century words. He may try to find technical, scientific understandings in simple, picturesque language. Symbolic portions of Scripture are especially prone to this abuse. This does not mean the symbolic language has no foundation in truth, but it may require considerable digging to uncover that foundation.

Proper interpretation. Proper interpretation must always consider what the original author meant to say to his original audience. The contexts of time and place are as important as the context of words. The admonition to "greet one another with a holy kiss" is best understood in the context of a time and place when kissing was a standard greeting (Luke 7:45). Any application made from that admonition today must center on the "holy," not the "kiss."

25

It is the authority of the whole Bible that makes proper interpretation possible. No part is "suspect." The Bible must be regarded as the best interpreter of itself; therefore, everything the Bible says on a certain subject must be considered in order to have the final word. If determination of authoritative and non-authoritative parts had to be included in the process, interpretation would become nothing but proof texting and reading into passages whatever one desired. The process would be subtle, even subconscious, but the only means of determing what in the Bible has authority would be subjective. Objective interpretation would be impossible.

Authority and Interpretation Inseparable

Discrepancies

So what about alleged discrepancies in the Bible? How can the whole of Scripture be authoritative when certain parts seem contradictory? The problem is, again, interpretation. If two passages seem to contradict, then the interpreter has not perceived the entire picture. Truth is harmonious with all truth.

This is the simple explanation based on what the Bible affirms for itself. Yet this is the great stumbling block. Scholars who hold the Bible in high regard are troubled by problems they cannot resolve. To admit that a Bible that is wholly inspired contradicts itself is to deny the authority of the whole Bible. Thus, they deny that the whole Bible is inspired in order to preserve the authority of part of the Bible. A better solution, however, is to admit that they simply do not have all of the facts. The Bible does not give complete information about every subject it introduces, but it gives sufficient information to accomplish its divine purpose.

The Relevance of Scripture

Every year schools discard thousands of textbooks and buy newer ones. The old ones are outdated, irrelevant. So why does the church continue with the same Bible? The version may change, but the Bible has remained essentially unchanged for nearly 2000 years. Can a book so old really be relevant to twentieth-century society?

The discussion of the relevance of Scripture is really an extension of the discussion of its authority. Does Scripture continue to have the same authority it once had, or do changes in time and culture require a new Word from God?

Relevance Depends on Authority

Timeliness

God has chosen to reveal His Word in timely fashion. His revelation was always intelligible to those who received it, at least to some extent. That seems at least part of the reason the Bible contains no textbook explanations of scientific material, for whose science would God use? Scientific explanations suitable to the twentieth century A.D. would have been utter nonsense ten centuries before Christ. And if the Lord tarries another twenty centuries, current scientific data will seem as primitive as stone-age science seems to us, if not more so. Thus, God spoke in the language of those to whom He spoke, and so did His messengers.

This highlights the importance of historical context in interpreting Scripture. Understanding the idolatrous habits of the Canaanites, for example, sheds light on God's commands for His people to remain separate from them. It even helps us understand His commands to annihilate certain cities. Although such commands embarrass some today, the action is not substantially different from the destruction of Sodom and Gomorrah. God merely used a different agent of executing judgment.

Timelessness

God's revelation is also timeless. Avoiding scientific language that becomes outdated, God reveals His truth in immortal terminology. To say the sun rises and sets is in harmony with the language of all times since the beginning until now. To say the earth revolves so that the sun shines on only half of it at a time is comparatively recent terminology. The former is not false, but is picturesque. Even we who know about the revolving earth are not afraid to speak of sunrise and sunset.

Not only the language, but the message as well is timeless. The answer to the question, "What must I do to be saved?" is the same today as it was in the first century. The Bible provides our answer in the answer to the crowds at Pentecost or to the Philippian jailer. The basic moral principles the Israelites were commanded to follow are applicable today as well.

A Timeless Message in Timeless Language

Audience

When we begin to get specific about the relevance of particular Biblical statements, the question of audience must be considered. Promises made to disciples in general are much more relevant to disciples today than those made specifically to the apostles. Jesus' promise in Acts 1:5, that the apostles would be baptized with the Holy Spirit, was specifically for the apostles, not all Christians. It is a mistake that ignores the evidence in the rest of Acts to believe the promise is broader than that. Jesus even gives the time the

28

promise would be fulfilled, obviously limiting the promise to a single event.

It is on a similar basis that many people propose great limitations to the relevance of Scripture. They suggest that since the Bible was written to certain people in a certain time, place, and culture, its relevance today is much weakened. Many of the injunctions imposed on Israel, for example, were to prevent them from adopting the false gods of their neighbors. While the pagan religious festivals included sexual activities, God prohibited fornication, homosexuality, incest, and the like. Since the problem of pagan influence no longer confronts us, some would suggest that these prohibitions are also irrelevant.

This reasoning does not always follow so radical a path. It generally goes around only those injuctions a person would like to live without. Thus, many who will not bypass God's prohibitions of sexual perversion will suggest that Paul's attitude toward women was cultural and irrelevant today. But while understanding the culture in which Paul spoke/ wrote is important in understanding his message, the application must transcend that culture. Some go so far as to say that such "cultural" ideas are not even inspired; they were merely each writer's opinion. We have already seen the problems that accompany that kind of thinking.

The real problem in any view of limited relevance is subjectivity. Whatever one does not wish to heed, he passes off as irrelevant. The real authority becomes the individual, not God. **Subjectivity the Enemy of Authority** Where Scripture does not specifically limit a command or principle by addressing it to a limited audience or referring to a specific time or circumstance, we dare not usurp God's authority and limit His commands.

One special note is in order here. What of those passages where Paul says he is giving his opinion (1 Corinthians 7:12, 25)? These are contrasted with his reference to specific instructions from the Lord (1 Corinthians 7:10). The solution is the difference between revelation and inspiration. Some things Paul knew by revelation; he received them directly from the Lord. The rest of what he wrote he knew by inspiration, that process by which God protected the writings of men who used their own minds to decide what to write. Thus, Paul's "opinion" is an inspired opinion, and, as such, has both authority and relevance for us today.

The Law and the Gospel

Of particular concern for Christians is the relevance of the Old Testament, the law, now that the gospel has been revealed. Some would deny the law's relevance, believing that since the gospel has come, we no longer need the "school master." Many of these people have problems with many New Testament commands, too, however. They want to believe that the gospel is just a matter of "love," not of "doctrine." They forget, however, that the apostles frequently used the Old Testament in their preaching, and Paul makes a very strong appeal for sound doctrine in his first letter to Timothy.

The traditional view is that the Old Testament is relevant and authoritative except where the New Testament supersedes it. There is some debate over whether precedent may supersede the Old Testament or command only (e.g., whether the meeting of the early church on the first day of the week nullifies the sabbath commands of the Old Testament), but the principle remains. Most who claim to hold that view, however, do not practice it. The Old Testament is largely neglected in the pulpit and in personal devotions. Parents recite the exciting Bible stories to their children, and the wisdom literature (especially the Psalms and Proverbs) receives a fair amount of attention, but the rest is largely neglected. How many sermons are preached from Leviticus?

Does NT Precedent Supersede OT Command?

The distinction between the law and the gospel must be seen as it really is. God has not changed His attitude toward sin. He has provided a new means of deliverance. Whereas the law taught salvation by works, the gospel teaches salvation by faith. Works are not unimportant in the New Testa-

30

ment, but they do not bring salvation. Nevertheless, it is well to note that the New Testament puts a high regard on works.

Thus, the Old Testament contains a wealth of information on how God views sin and on how we should conduct ourselves. The New Testa- **Old & New** ment provides our motive (faith), and the **Testaments Complementary** Old Testament provides some specifics in regard to proper conduct. The ritual of the Old Testament is gone, along with the sacrifices and the priesthood. But the concept of sin and God's attitude toward sin remains. We can learn much from the study of the Old Testament.

Conclusion

Revelation, inspiration, authority, and relevance. They are so closely related that they stand or fall together. If God has revealed His will to man, then it has His authority, and is relevant to all ages. If God has chosen to inspire a book so that people in all ages can know His will, then that book also bears His authority and is relevant in all ages. The Bible claims to be such a book.

We can depend on the Bible to provide God's revelation of himself. Through the inspiration of God's Spirit, men of God have committed that revelation to writing. We do not worship a book; we worship God, who is revealed in that book. But that book is our only authoritative revelation of the God we worship.

As we read and understand the Bible, we understand God's will for us. And if we claim to follow the Lord, then we consider what the Bible says to have authority and relevance for us. God speaks to us through the Bible. We dare not "nullify the word of God" (Matthew 15:3-6) by clever interpretation or any other "tradition." We are obliged to obey.

31

5

The Old Testament

After even a superficial examination of the Old Testament Scriptures, it becomes obvious that God did **Progressive Revelation** not drop His entire scheme of redemption upon man at once. In human experience, an infant is not capable of receiving nearly as much information as a first-grader. And only when adulthood has been reached is the individual able to cope, on his own, with all of the experiences that go along with being a social and reasonable creation. The human race as a whole has been no different. This process of maturation necessitated what is known as "progressive revelation." God spoke "at many times and in various ways" (Hebrews 1:1), here a little, there a little, until man had reached the point where the climactic revelation in Christ would be comprehensible.

Thus, the Old Testament records the plans of God for His creation from the first simple commands to the original pair, through the directives of God to Abraham and his grandson Israel, through the expression of God's will in the law of Moses, to the message of the prophets forecasting the coming of the ultimate redemption in Christ. To accomplish His purpose in this pre-Christian Testament, God allowed the writers to use several different forms or categories of literature.

The Old Testament Divisions

Most Christians who have grown up in Sunday School are familiar with the divisions of the Old Testament in the English Bible: five books of law, twelve of history, five of poetry, and seventeen of prophecy. While these divisions are, for the most part, descriptive of the contents of each, it is also true that there is a great deal of overlapping. In other words, much in the books of law is history; a large portion of the prophetic books is poetic literature. Thus, other classifications are possible. It seems appropriate to see how the Hebrew people themselves divided the writings in their Scriptures.

The first division was the *Torah*. This is the Hebrew word for "law," and it comprises the same five books as our books of law. This section is also known as the Pentateuch.

Three Hebrew Divisions

The tradition, both Jewish and Christian, has held Moses to be the author of these books. This tradition has stood unchallenged until comparatively recent times. However, there is sufficient evidence in the Scripture to support this traditional view of authorship. We are told that Moses "wrote down everything the Lord had said" (Exodus 24:4, 7). The "law" is said to have been written by Moses (Deuteronomy 31:9, 24-26). The historical sections are also said to be written by Moses on two occasions (Exodus 17:14; Numbers 33:1, 2); the "Song of Moses" is attributed to his authorship (Deuteronomy 31:19). The last of the prophets cites "the law of . . . Moses" (Malachi 4:4), and Jesus refers to Exodus as "the book of Moses" (Mark 12:26). Jesus not only considers Moses the one through whom the law was given, but also the one who wrote it down (Mark 10:5). The Lord's brother James refers to Moses' being "read in the synagogues on every Sabbath" (Acts 15:21), and the inspired apostle Paul also refers to the reading of Moses by the Jews (2 Corinthians 3:15).

Thus, while Mosaic authorship is denied as impossible by modern critical scholarship, the internal evidence, tradition, and other Scriptural references support it. There is no irrefutable reason compelling one to discard the Mosaic authorship of the Torah. The time of writing would then be about 1400 B.C.

The second division of the Hebrews' Bible was that known as the *Prophets*. This section included not only most

33

of what we know as the major and minor prophets, but several of the books of history, as well.

In this section, the book of Joshua was certainly written by a contemporary of the events narrated therein (Joshua 5:1; 6:25), and Jewish and Christian tradition has ascribed it to Joshua himself. The book of Judges was written when the Jebusites still held Jerusalem (Judges 1:21), but they were eliminated by King David. Also, the writer says that "in those days, Israel had no king" (Judges 21:25), implying that there was a king when the writing was done. Thus, it must have been written during the time of Saul, and Samuel is declared to be the author by Hebrew tradition. The two books of Samuel refer to a division between Israel and Judah (1 Samuel 27:6), leading some to suggest a late date for the book. However, the distinction existed even before the split after Solomon's death (2 Samuel 2:10). Thus, there is no reason to question the tradition that Samuel wrote to the time of his death (1 Samuel 25:1), and that Nathan probably wrote the rest. The Talmud states that Jeremiah was the author of the books of kings, and rabbinical tradition holds that he wrote 2 Kings 25:27-30 as an old man in Babylon, taken there when Nebuchadnezzar conquered Egypt in 568 B.C.

The unity of Isaiah's prophecy has been denied by some during the last two centuries; however, the twenty-five previous centuries point virtually unanimously to Isaiah as the author of the entire book, writing in the eighth century before Christ. The book of Jeremiah is likewise named for its author, who dictated much of his prophecy to his secretary, Baruch (Jeremiah 36:1-4) in the sixth century before Christ. The inspired apostle Matthew quotes Jeremiah 31:15, and attributes the quotation to the prophet Jeremiah (Matthew 2:18). Much of the book of Ezekiel is written in the first person, pointing to the prophet Ezekiel himself as the author in the early sixth century B.C. His name is even used in Ezekiel 1:2 and 24:24. He was a priest (Ezekiel 1:2) who was carried captive to Babylon (Ezekiel 1:1).

Hosea was another eighth century prophet, contemporary with Isaiah, and he wrote the book that bears his name. The book of Joel was evidently written by "Joel son of Pethuel" (1:1), in the late ninth century B.C. A shepherd of Tekoa, Amos, is identified as the source of the book bearing his name (1:1). Obadiah allows himself to slip into the background, not identifying himself in the book; but evidently the book was named for its author. The evidence for the prophet Jonah's authorship of the book bearing his name is found in Josephus and in the apocryphal book of Tobit. Micah of Moresheth identifies himself in Micah 1:1; he was a contemporary of Isaiah. The book of Nahum is credited to Nahum the Elkoshite (Nahum 1:1), who wrote in the seventh century B.C. Habakkuk likewise identifies himself (Habakkuk 1:1), again writing in the late seventh century. Zephaniah gives a lengthy pedigree for himself (Zephaniah 1:1), showing that he was a descendant of King Hezekiah. He wrote in the late seventh century. Haggai was a contemporary of Zechariah, and they both wrote in the late sixth century. Finally, although the Hebrew word *malachi* in Malachi 1:1 may be translated either by a proper name, Malachi, or by the word's meaning, "my messenger," the Jewish tradition has held from the earliest times that this book was written by a man named Malachi in the late fifth century.

The third division in the Hebrew Bible is known as the *Kethuvim,* or the *Writings.* These writings are sometimes referred to as the *Hagiographa,* the Greek word for "holy writings." Standing at the head of this division are the

Psalms a National Hymnal

Psalms, which form the hymnal for the nation of Israel. In the titles, seventy-three are ascribed to David, twelve to Asaph, eleven to the sons of Korah, two to Solomon, one to Moses, and one to Ethan; the other fifty have no designated author. The writing of the Psalms extended over nearly a millennium, one being written by Moses (Psalm 90; fifteenth century), and one during the Babylonian exile (Psalm 137; sixth century).

35

The book of Job has traditionally been ascribed to Moses, written while he was in Midian. This would make it the oldest book of the Bible. The book of Proverbs is claimed by Solomon in Proverbs 1:1 (see also 10:1; 25:1). The names given in chapters thirty and thirty-one are generally viewed as other names for Solomon, although they may have been other inspired men otherwise unknown.

The *Megilloth,* or rolls, were five books, each of which was short enough to be read on a special occasion. The book of Ruth was read during the Feast of Weeks, or Pentecost. The Talmud ascribes the book to Samuel, who anointed David and thus would know of his popularity (Ruth 4:22). Song of Solomon was read at the great feast of Passover. It claims to be by Solomon (Song of Solomon 1:1). Ecclesiastes was read during the Feast of Tabernacles, and was written by the king in Jerusalem (Ecclesiastes 1:12), and the son of David the king (Ecclesiastes 1:1). Thus, it was ascribed unanimously to Solomon, until the time of Luther. There is no evidence in the book to discredit this ascription. The book of Lamentations was read on the anniversary of the burning of the temple. The tradition, Jewish and Christian, has said that Jeremiah was the author. The scroll of Esther was read at the Feast of Purim, which was instituted in the time recorded in this book. No author is mentioned, but Mordecai recorded all the events (Esther 9:20); so he may be the one the Lord inspired to write the canonical book.

Special Scrolls for Special Occasions

The book of Daniel presents the Jewish captive who became a chief administrator in Persia as the author of the book (Daniel 8:1ff). The Lord Jesus affirms this in His Olivet discourse (Matthew 24:15). In the Hebrew Bible, Ezra and Nehemiah were considered to be one book. Ezra was ascribed in the Talmud to that fifth century writer, while the first person pronoun in Nehemiah, used to refer to Nehemiah himself, leaves no doubt as to the author. The authorship of the books of Chronicles, considered one book by the Jews, is given in the Talmud as Ezra.

In this brief survey, we have seen the three divisions in the Hebrew Bible: the Torah, the Prophets, and the Writings. It has not been our purpose to discuss all the questions that are focused on the various books, but to give the best conclusions regarding their authors, usually suggested by the books themselves. Whereas this is too brief for much scholarly use, it is hoped that such a survey will prove helpful for the average reader and Bible student.

The Languages of the Old Testament

The Old Testament was written in two distinct but related languages. In addition, a third language is extremely significant for our study, although it was not one of the original languages of the authors of the books.

By far, the vast majority of the Old Testament was written in Hebrew. This was the language of the ancient Hebrew people. During the period of the Divided kingdom, it began to be replaced by Aramaic. By the first century A.D., Hebrew was essentially the language of the scholars. After the founding of the state of Israel in 1948, however, Hebrew was revived as a living language and is now the national tongue of that state.

Hebrew is a dynamic language, emphasing action. Its alphabet contains twenty-two characters, which can be seen at the beginning of the sections of Psalm 119 in most translations. The beauty of Hebrew lies in its simplicity. **Hebrew a Dynamic, Simple Language** There are only about five thousand different words in the Old Testament, and nine tenths of these are used only a few times. A line is read from right to left, and a book is read from back to front. The ability to read this language opens the text in a way that makes the writings of Moses, David, and the others come alive with new meaning.

The Aramaic language is found in just a few places in the Old Testament: Daniel 2:4b—7:28; Ezra 4:8—6:18; 7:12-26; Jeremiah 10:11; and the name of *Jegar Sahadutha* in Genesis 31:47. Because this was the language spoken in first-century Palestine, there are also Aramaic words found in the New Testament, such as the word *Abba* in Romans 8:15, or the words *Talitha cumi* in Mark 5:41.

The third important language is Greek. Although the Old Testament was not written in Greek, many Jewish people were settled in areas that spoke this language after the conquests of Alexander the Great (356-323 B.C.). In about 280 B.C., Ptolemy II Philadelphus received a request from the curator of the great library in Alexandria, Egypt, to have the Hebrew law in the collection. He obtained seventy-two Jewish translators, who rendered the Pentateuch into Greek. In the succeeding years, the rest of the Old Testament and fourteen apocryphal books written in Hebrew and Greek were added to the version of the Bible translated into the latter language. This translation came to be known as the *Septuagint,* because a legend maintained that the entire Old Testament was translated in seventy days. It is usually designated by the abbreviation LXX, the Roman numerals for seventy. The fourteen apocryphal books, though not considered Scripture by the Jews themselves, were included in the Latin Vulgate translation of the Bible; so they are counted as Scripture by the Roman Catholic Church.

The importance of this Greek translation lies in its frequent quotation by New Testament writers. **Septuagint Often Quoted in NT** There are enough textual differences between the Septuagint and the Hebrew that it is generally easy for a competent scholar to determine from which the quotation came. It is clear that the Christian church accepted the Septuagint as faithfully rendering the Word of God. This very acceptance led the Jews to cast off the translation, and thus, with few exceptions, the only copies we possess of the Septuagint are Christian copies.

The Septuagint also helps us get back to the original Hebrew. It was translated in the third century B.C. from current Hebrew manuscripts. The oldest Hebrew manuscripts now available to us are from the first or second century A.D. Granted, we do not have the original Septuagint, but what we have is still helpful.

38

6

The New Testament

The writing of the New Testament has preserved for us God's ultimate revelation, His revelation through Jesus Christ. It is so readily accessible today that it is somewhat taken for granted. But that revelation was not always so easy to get. At first, the apostles dedicated themselves to the "ministry of the word of God" (Acts 6:2) and everyone in the church had audible access to the Word. But as "the word of God spread" (Acts 6:7), so did the church, and not everyone could hear an apostle or other eyewitness of the gospel events. A written record was needed.

The Gospels

Matthew's Gospel was written first, and Revelation last, but the rest of the New Testament did not come chronologically as they are arranged in between. Matthew wrote his Gospel in about A.D. 45,* perhaps first in Hebrew and then in Greek. Some of the second century writers allude to a Hebrew "Matthew," but the only copies that remain today are Greek. Matthew did write to a primarily Jewish audience. He goes to some length to demonstrate that Jesus fulfilled the Old Testament rather than contradicted it. That is the reason he so often quotes the Old Testament (more than sixty times). His Gospel became an evangelistic tool for Jews and an apologetic (defense of the faith) tool for Jewish Christians.

NT Not Arranged Chronologically

*Dates assigned in this chapter are based on Henry C. Thiessen, *Introduction to the New Testament* (Grand Rapids: Eerdmans, 1943) and Lewis A. Foster, class lectures, "New Testament Survey" (Cincinnati: Cincinnati Bible College, 1975).

Mark's Gospel appeared about A.D. 65, its author largely influenced by the preaching fo the apostle Peter. He may also have been an eyewitness of some of the events, however. He is the only one to record the incident of the young man in the Garden of Gethsemane (Mark 14:51, 52), which prompts some scholars to believe Mark was that young man. He wrote primarily for the Romans, who had begged him to write the Gospel. The Romans were an active people, and that explains the action character of Mark's Gospel. He uses the term "immediately" over forty times, four times as many as the other Gospels combined. This also explains why his is the shortest Gospel.

Luke a Gentile Writer

Luke was the only Gentile to write a Gospel. He was not an eyewitness of the events, but "carefully investigated everything from the beginning" (Luke 1:3). He mentions other accounts that were circulating (Luke 1:1), but he seems to have relied more on the eyewitness accounts of the apostles ("servants of the word," Luke 1:2) than on these other accounts. He wrote for Theophilus specifically (Luke 1:3) and Greeks generally. His account is the most "historical" in our sense of the word, as he was the best educated of the Gospel writers. Luke wrote his Gospel before he wrote Acts (Acts 1:1, 2), which he seems to have concluded just at the end of Paul's two-year imprisonment in Rome (Acts 28:30). Thus, the Gospel was probably written in about A.D. 60.

These three Gospels, Matthew, Mark, and Luke, are called the "Synoptic Gospels" because they are very similar to one another. This has caused some scholars to propose "sources" and copying for the writing of these accounts, but any such theory questions inspiration. Most, though certainly not all, who believe such theories do not even believe the Gospels were written by first-century authors. But no evidence exists to dispute the authenticity of the Synoptic Gospels. Matthew, an eyewitness, obviously needed no sources. Mark, possibly an eyewitness and a companion of Peter, likewise needed no sources. Luke also claims to have used eyewitness testimony in his work. Add to this the inspiration of the Holy Spirit, and no copying or "source theories" need to be suggested.

John's Gospel was written much later, about A.D. 90, and is much different than the Synoptics. John seems to have been aware of the character of the other Gospels; so he deliberately took a different approach. His is a **John's Gospel Deliberately Different** more "spiritual" or philosophical Gospel. He was "the disciple whom Jesus loved," and this special relationship is probably the background for the special insight shown in his Gospel. It is a more universal Gospel, not written specifically for Jews (though he himself was a Jew and his style is obviously Jewish), Romans, or Greeks, but for the whole church. By the time he wrote, the church had spread throughout the known world, and his Gospel was accepted everywhere.

Acts

"The Acts of the Apostles" is a bit of a misnomer, for the book does not attempt to give all the acts of all the apostles. It focuses mainly on Peter (chapters 1-12) and Paul (chapters 13-28). It picks up where the author, Luke, left off with his Gospel and traces the history of the church to the close of Paul's first Roman imprisonment in A.D. 63. It tells of Jesus' commission to the apostles to be His "witnesses in Jerusalem, and in all Judea and Samaria, and to the ends of the earth." It also tells how that commission was accomplished: chapters 1-7 tell about the church in Jerusalem, chapters 8-12 tell of the spread of the church into Judea and Samaria, and the remainder of the book tells how the church advanced throughout the world as far as Rome—the capital of the empire.

The man who seems to have done the most to advance the church worldwide was Paul. He did it by traveling on what we call missionary journeys and by writing letters. Several of those letters are preserved for us in the New Testament.

The Epistles (Letters)

Paul's first letter was written at Corinth to the Thessalonians in A.D. 52. Paul was on his sec-
Paul Wrote ond missionary journey and had already
to Correct preached in Thessalonica, and Timothy had
Problems been sent back to that city. Timothy's return
to Paul in Corinth was not entirely happy, for it prompted
Paul to write 1 Thessalonians. Apparently, Timothy had
reported that some of the Thessalonians had misunderstood
Paul's teaching on the second coming and had given up
work, waiting for Jesus' return. There were other problems,
as well, and Paul wrote to the Thessalonians to deal with all
those problems.

Second Thessalonians was written later in the same year.
This explains the similarity of the two books (for example,
why Paul again addressed the issue of the second coming
and how to prepare for it). The situation was very similar,
having not had time to change significantly. Apparently,
there continued to be much confusion, and Paul feared the
situation would worsen unless he again intervened.

On his third missionary journey, Paul wrote four great
letters, including his most popular, 1 Corinthians and Romans. These are Paul's longest letters and naturally contain
more material than any of his other books; thus, their use is
wider in the church. They treat more subjects more com-
prehensively than any other of his writings.

First Corinthians was written from Ephesus in A.D. 57.
The Corinthians had written Paul a letter asking him various
questions about proper conduct in their new relationship
with Christ. In addition, Paul had heard from other sources
that grave problems were brewing in Corinth; so he wrote
them this letter. It reads like a catalog of problems and
answers, dealing with factions, incest, lawsuits, fornication,
marriage, Christian liberty, worship and order, and the resurrection. Yet, one theme runs throughout the book—that
of Christian unity. All the issues discussed have bearing on
the problem of unity within the church.

Second Corinthians was written later that same year or

early in 58. Paul had sent Titus to Corinth to discover how the first letter was received. He was so anxious for an answer that he left Ephesus in order to meet Titus as he was returning to Paul (2 Corinthians 2:12, 13). He met Titus in Macedonia and received good news (2 Corinthians 7:5-7). The Corinthians had learned some painful lessons, but they were making progress. Some problems remained, particularly an attack on Paul's authority. Apparently the party spirit was dissolving, and those who still held it were having to be more vehement in their attacks. Thus, in some ways, things might appear to have worsened. But it was a vocal minority; most of the church was making progress. Paul wrote to rejoice in the progress and to encourage those who remained divisive to heed his authority.

The letter to the Galatians was written shortly after 2 Corinthians, and about a similar problem. In it Paul defended his apostolic ministry against divisive persons who claimed he was inferior to other apostles. Here, the problem was caused by "Judaizers," Jews who claimed that Gentiles must become Jews and follow the law to be Christians.

So far, Paul's letters had been to churches he himself founded. Romans is different. Paul had been wanting to visit Rome for some time (Romans 1:13), but at the time he wrote them in A.D. 58, he had been unable to do **Paul Wrote to Prevent Problems** so. His letter was intended to convey his wishes and to prepare for such a visit. But there is much more to the letter than that. The church at Rome seems to have started without any apostolic leadership. Although the church seemed strong at the time, Paul was concerned about this lack of leadership, especially since the Judaizers were causing so much trouble elsewhere. They claimed to have apostolic authority (Acts 15:24), and if they reached the church at Rome, they could certainly wreak havoc. So Paul wrote the Romans from Corinth to prevent problems before they could arise.

Acts tells us that Paul did finally reach Rome, but it was as a prisoner. During the two years he was there in prison, he was able to have visitors, he preached, and he wrote letters. The "prison epistles," Colossians, Philemon, Ephesians, and Philippians, were written during this time. They were probably written near the end of his imprisonment in A.D. 63, as his absence was beginning to be felt more strongly. His references of visits to Philemon (Philemon 22) and the Philippians (Philippians 2:24) indicate that he expected to be released soon.

The Judaizers were continuing to cause problems in the churches. In Colosse, they teamed up with a "gnostic" group. (Gnosticism is a speculative religion that elevates knowledge and the non-material, considering anything material to be evil.) Thus Paul wrote to them of the gospel and deliverance from the law, and "hollow and deceptive philosophy" (Colossians 2:8). He closed with recommendations for Tychicus, who was returning to Colosse with the letter and would be leading the church in applying what Paul had written.

Judaizers & Gnostics Caused Trouble

Accompanying Tychicus was Onesimus, a runaway slave of Philemon, a resident of Colosse. Paul had converted Onesimus in Rome, and sent him home. The letter to Philemon was intended to encourage Philemon to welcome his slave back as a brother.

Paul wrote to the Ephesians, also, concerning the same problems he wrote about in the Colossian letter. In fact, the two have many parallel passages. But he seems to be writing prevention rather than cure, for his tone is much softer and less harsh. He sent it also with Tychicus, as Colosse and Ephesus were fairly close.

Philippians is a thank-you letter. Paul and the Philippians shared a special relationship. The church had sent Epaphroditus to Rome to "take care of" Paul's needs (Philippians 2:25). He had apparently been there for some time, long enough to get sick, almost to the point of death, and for the Philippians to find out about it (Philippians 2:26, 27). Paul was sending him back with this letter of gratitude and encouragement to remain faithful. It is quite possible that

44

Epaphroditus came to Rome shortly after Paul was imprisoned there, and remained until the apostle's release seemed imminent.

After his release, Paul again began traveling and wrote three letters known as the "pastoral epistles." These were written to young evangelists he had trained and had sent to churches he himself could not visit. Two of them, 1 Timothy and Titus, were written at about the same time, A.D. 65, and for the same purpose. They contain such information as how to deal with false teachers, appoint elders and deacons, and teach sound doctrine. Each one also contains some personal instructions for the specific situation.

Pastorals Written After Paul's Release

The third, 2 Timothy, was written from a Roman prison one or two years later. It is a letter of encouragement to, perhaps, Paul's closest friend. Paul was not expecting release this time, but death. Though he faced death confidently, he felt a need to see Timothy again, and requested that he come and bring Paul's cloak and scrolls. Paul was not released, but, according to tradition, was executed in A.D. 67, making 2 Timothy his last letter.

The identity of the writer of Hebrews remains a mystery, but it was likely written by Paul. It lacks his characteristic opening, but it is addressed to a Jewish audience, who might have been prejudiced against a letter starting with, "Paul, an apostle. . . ." Much in the book is similar to Paul's letters, such as his emphasis on faith, and the author was at some time a companion of Timothy (Hebrews 13:23). It was written from Rome (Hebrews 13:24), possibly from Paul's first imprisonment in A.D. 63.

The letters that were written by James, Peter, John, and Jude are called "general epistles." They were not written to specific churches or individuals, but to Christians in general in particular areas. (The books of 2 John and 3 John are specifically addressed, but they are included as general epistles because of 1 John.)

James, the Lord's half-brother, wrote to Jewish Christians

45

scattered throughout the eastern part of the empire in A.D. 62. James was highly respected in Jerusalem, serving as spokesman for the apostles and elders at the Jerusalem Conference in A.D. 50 (Acts 15:13-21). He wrote of proper conduct for Christians, particularly in the face of persecution. His emphasis on conduct, or "works," has often been challenged as more Jewish than Christian, and at variance with Paul's emphasis on "faith." However, the two views are not contradictory but complementary. Each considers the same concept from a different viewpoint, but those viewpoints are harmonious. Paul says Abraham was justified by faith (Romans 4); James says by works (James 2:21-24). The fact is, Abraham was justified by a faith that worked, for "faith by itself, if it is not accompanied by action, is dead" (James 2:17).

The apostle Peter wrote two letters to Christians scattered throughout the Roman empire. Writing **Encouragement for Persecuted Christians** from Rome, he wrote his first letter to encourage the believers in the face of mounting opposition and persecution. Surprisingly, his audience seems to be predominantly Gentile rather than Jewish. Their problems are more closely related to the pagan Gentile influence than to Judaizers. Another surprise is the role of Silas in the writing (1 Peter 5:12). Silas is more often thought of in connection with Paul than with Peter. Peter also mentions Mark, whom he calls his son (1 Peter 5:13). Origen says Peter's reference is a result of Mark's Gospel, which reproduced Peter's preaching. This would date 1 Peter just after the Gospel of Mark, about A.D. 65 or 66. Peter's second letter was written to the same audience very shortly after the first. It is a warning against false teachers and an encouragement to grow in Christian character.

Jude, like James, was a half-brother of the Lord. He wrote a warning against false teachers, as did Peter, but to the Jewish audience of his brother. Much in his letter is very similar to 2 Peter, which he may have been quoting. He wrote it in about A.D. 75.

46

The apostle John wrote his three letters very shortly after he wrote his Gospel, in A.D. 90. The first is truly general, perhaps addressed to the same seven churches as Revelation (Revelation 2, 3); 2 John is addressed to a Christian woman, now unknown to us, who perhaps hosted a church in her home; and 3 John is written to Gaius, of whom we know virtually nothing. The name is common enough that it cannot be positively linked with any other Gaius in Scripture. The first letter is an appeal of love to resist false teaching. The prominence of "love" in the letter brings to mind John's reference to himself in his Gospel, "the disciple whom Jesus loved." He seems to have learned much from Jesus' example. Second John, much shorter than 1 John, is a condensed version of the former letter. Love and a warning of false teachers are its theme. Third John is a personal letter, commending Gaius for his hospitality.

Revelation

The last book of the New Testament, the Revelation of John, was written in A.D. 96. During a period of exile on the island of Patmos, *Apocalypse,* an John received this revelation and delivered Uncovering it to the church. The style is partially the same as an epistle or letter, at least for the first three chapters. As such, it is addressed to seven churches in Asia Minor with whom John had a close relationship. The rest of the book is "apocalyptic," which means "an uncovering." It is more than just prophecy of future events or the end of time. "Apocalypse" was a special literary style and was highly figurative. As such, the book warrants very special care in interpretation.

Even so, the book ought not to be considered impossible to understand. It is an "uncovering," not a mystery without solution. It was written to encourage Christians in a time of persecution, written by a "companion in the suffering." It is a declaration of victory for the Lord's side. Any interpretation of the book must keep that in mind.

7

The Collection of the Old Testament

The writing of the Bible took hundreds of years, and perhaps none of its authors was aware he was writing a "Bible." The individual books were written for individual reasons, as we have seen in the preceding chapters. So what caused the books to be collected into the Bible as we know it? Why these books and why not others?

The Canon

The term *canon* comes from a Greek word for a "measuring rod." Since about 300 years after Christ, the term has been used for the collection of books regarded as Scripture. The idea is that those books "measure up" to the standard required of Scripture. This does not mean, however, that there was no Bible until that time. There was no canon committee that met to determine which books would be canonical. Just as a rose by any other name would smell as sweet, so the canon by any other name would still measure up. And the writings included in our Bibles today have been accepted since the time of their writing, even though it was quite some time before they were called the "canon."

Canon Measures Up

The Old Testament canon has been the source of some debate. The arrangement of the books varies widely in the different manuscripts. There is even a question over the divisions of the Hebrew Bible; the three divisions previously mentioned do not occur in all manuscripts. Many have but

48

two divisions: the law and the prophets. In fact, Jesus most often referred to the Old Testament by this designation, as in Matthew 22:40 and Luke 16:16. Only once did He imply a three-way division: the law, the prophets, and the psalms (Luke 24:44). Psalms here represents all the books now called the writings, for it is the most prominent in that division.

Much has been made of these differences—much more than is justified. They do not suggest that some of the books were not accepted immediately, or that they were only partially accepted. The fact that Jesus referred to both methods of division makes that clear. The simple explanation is based on the fact that these books were written on scrolls. As such, they could be arranged differently for different occasions. The two-way division seems to be the original division, with a third division being made for use in synagogue worship services. The expression, "the law and the prophets," makes clear what the Jews thought of the inspiration of their sacred writings, and the three-way division ought not to be looked on as a denial of inspiration for part of the books.

Different Arrangements for Different Purposes

Collecting the Books

The law. Efforts were made immediately to collect and preserve the law of Moses. The stone tablets on which God had written were kept in the ark of the covenant (Exodus 40:20). Later, "Moses wrote down this law" and entrusted it to the Levites with the command that it be read every seven years to the whole nation of Israel (Deuteronomy 31:9-12). Joshua even received God's own testimony on the authority of the law of Moses (Joshua 1:1-8), and was ordered not to let it "depart" from his mouth.

The "law" continued to be kept by the priests in the temple. During the time of the divided kingdom, evil kings ignored the law and led the people into idolatry. The law was still preserved in the temple, however. After the nation of Israel had fallen, Judah was left in a pitiable condition.

49

The temple in Jerusalem was falling apart from neglect and abuse. Finally, King Josiah ordered that the temple be repaired, and it was then that the high priest Hilkiah "found" the book of the law (2 Kings 22:8). Its discovery led to a national revival, for the king and other godly men recognized it as the Word of God.

The prophets. Designating the Old Testament as "the law and the prophets" indicates why the Old Testament books were collected. Moses' writings, the law, were believed to be inspired because Moses had such intimate contact with God. The rest of the writings were believed to be inspired because they were written by "prophets," that is, inspired men. Thus, as new books were written, they were accepted and added to the canon.

All OT Books Written by Prophets

There is evidence within the historical books that they were immediately accepted and added to the collection. Joshua 24:25, 26 says that the "decrees and laws" written by Joshua were recorded in "the Book of the Law of God." Whether this means the entire book of Joshua was thus added to the canon might be debated, but something was added—something written by Joshua was accorded the same status as the writings of Moses.

The end of the book of Joshua was obviously written by someone else, for it records his death. Apparently the book was kept after Joshua had died, and someone added the closing. If the book were not valued as Scripture, it's doubtful anyone would have done this. The opening of the book of Judges reviews some of the history in Joshua, including the death of Joshua, obviously tying the two books together. It is likely that the author of Judges finished Joshua and proceeded to write the continued history of Israel.

A similar link is found between Ruth and 1 Samuel. (Ruth, in the Hebrew original, seems to have been part of the same book as Judges; so a link between Ruth and 1 Samuel is also a link between Judges and 1 Samuel.) Although there is no review in 1 Samuel, the setting is the time of the judges. Ruth, however, closed with a geneology extending into the reign of Saul by announcing the birth of David. This is quite natural if, as we have supposed, Samuel was the author of Judges, Ruth, and 1 Samuel. If Samuel did not write all of Judges and Ruth, it is highly likely that he added Judges 21:25 and the closing verses of Ruth. Thus, he added his approval to them just as Joshua had done with the law and as the author of Judges had done with Joshua.

Ezra makes an amazing connection with 2 Chronicles. The first two and one-half verses of Ezra are identical with the closing of the last two verses of 2 Chronicles. There is evidence that Ezra added the closing to 2 Chronicles in order to tie the two books together. Thus, at least for the historical section, there is strong evidence that the writers expected their writings to be preserved, just as the previous books had been preserved. Since the books were written on scrolls, it might be easy to get the order confused. These links, however, served to insure that Israel's history was preserved in the proper sequence.

Historical Books Linked in Sequence

The seventeen books that are called prophecy today were written by prophets in the "official" sense, and were obviously collected for that reason. That leaves only the poetry or wisdom literature needing comment. If Job was written by Moses, then it would naturally be held in high esteem and kept by the Jews. The psalms were written by several authors from Moses to exiled Jews. David wrote most of them. They were no doubt kept primarily for their value in worship services, but the authors were also regarded as inspired. This was not just a hymn book in the sense that we have hymn books today. Solomon wrote the remaining three books, and the source and extent of his wisdom is recorded in 1 Kings 3:5-14 and 1 Kings 4:29-34. His writing would naturally be collected by devout Jews.

The Apocrypha

There were other books written during the time that the Old Testament was written, but these books have not generally been accepted as Scripture. They are called the Apocrypha, from the Greek word meaning "obscure" or "hidden away." They are called this because they are of "obscure" origin; they are not known to be prophetic and are, thus, not accepted as Scripture.

These fourteen books are not found in the Hebrew manuscripts, but they are in the Septuagint. The Jews rejected them as Scripture, but found them useful as supplementary history and exposition, just as we today find secular writings useful.

We might ask, why are these not accepted? Indeed, the Roman Catholic Church does accept eleven of them, as a quick glance at the contents page of a Douay Bible will demonstrate. Their position is based on the Septuagint. Since the New Testament writers often quoted the Septuagint, the whole Septuagint is believed to have inspired approval. Jude also quoted one of these books, Enoch (Jude 14), and this is cited as further evidence.

The Jude quotation, however, is inconclusive. Paul quoted pagan authors (1 Corinthians 15:33; Titus 1:12), but this hardly grants them inspired status! Jude could likewise quote a secular source without accepting it as Scriptural. The argument based on the Septuagint has at least a couple of problems. First, the earliest copies of the Septuagint currently available (extant) are from at least the third century. These may or may not be identical with those in use in the first century. The New Testament authors may well have quoted a Septuagint that did not contain the Apocrypha. Second, since the New Testament was written in Greek, it was natural for the writers to quote the Greek Bible, the Septuagint. They did not necessarily endorse the whole Septuagint—if it differed from the Hebrew Bible—by quoting the Greek version.

Inspired Quotations—Not Inspired Sources

All the evidence from the first two centuries opposes the acceptance of the Apocrypha. Secular writers, quoting Scripture frequently, almost totally ignore it. The New Testament, quoting nearly every book of the Old Testament, has but one specific reference to the Apocrypha, and that need not be considered an acceptance as canonical. We may, with the Jews contemporary with the Apocrypha, appreciate its secular value yet deny its Scriptural validity.

Canonical Synods

For several years, now, a theory of a three-stage, formal process of establishing the canon has been popular. Those who believe this theory believe there were three council meetings, or synods, in which scholars discussed whether or not certain books belonged in the canon. At the heart of this theory is a denial of traditionally assigned authorship and dating of the books. Frequently, this charge is made so as to deny inspiration. For example, a book that predicts an event is dated after the event to give the author historical, rather than prophetic, knowledge of the event.

The law is believed to have been canonized at about 400 B.C. It was supposedly written by at least four authors, and was put together in the mid fourth century. The prophets are believed to have been canonized about 200 B.C., having been written only after the law was canonized. The writings, finally, are believed to have been canonized at the Synod of Jamnia in A.D. 90.

Liberal Theory of Canonization

The Synod of Jamnia is the only actual "synod" or meeting that is identified. The others are mere conjecture made to fit the theory. What happened at Jamnia, however, is not certain. There is no proof that all the writings were discussed or what the importance of the discussion really was.

As for the books themselves, many were accepted and quoted by contemporary writers before the dates given above. Recent manuscript discoveries are making the late dates assigned to some of the books very hard to live with, and this strains the theory terribly. It seems safer to accept a more traditional view of earlier writing with immediate "canonization."

The Collection of the New Testament

The national structure of Israel made the collection of the Old Testament books relatively easy. The prophetic writings had national significance, and the whole nation was interested in their preservation. The early church was different (as it obviously still is). The prophetic writings were usually addressed to specific congregations or individuals. There was no "nation" to collect these writings; so it was longer before they began to be used by the whole church.

These writings did begin to circulate, at least in a limited way, very early. Paul urged the Colossians **Circulation Began Early** to have the letter written to them "also read in the church of the Laodiceans" and to read "the letter from Laodicea" (Colossians 4:16). The Laodicean letter is presumably a letter from Paul to the Laodiceans that would be forwarded to the Colossians. Ephesians is generally regarded as a "cyclical" letter, that is, a letter intended to be circulated around to several churches before ending up in Ephesus. It may even be the "letter from Laodicea" mentioned in Colossians.

Several other of Paul's letters must have been circulated rather widely as well. Peter, writing in 65 or 66, already was familiar with several of Paul's letters, for he was able to refer to Paul's style "in all his letters" (2 Peter 3:16). Apparently, the churches that owned letters from Paul and other inspired writers would share the letters with other churches nearby. These letters were valuable, and were treasured by the churches that possessed them.

54

Copying

At some point, the inspired writings began to be copied. This was, at first, quite limited because of the time and expense involved. Paper was hand-made, usually from papyrus reeds, and was thus in short supply and expensive. Each copy had to be done by hand, slowly and carefully.

In spite of the expense, some of the writings were copied and circulated very early. John wrote his Gospel in A.D. 90, and archeologists have discovered fragments of a copy of his Gospel made in about A.D. 150. John wrote in Ephesus, and the copy was discovered in Egypt. Thus, John's Gospel was copied and widely circulated almost immediately.

Part of the reason for John's early acceptance, no doubt, is his late writing. His writings are the latest of all the canonical books. Other inspired writers had already died. The church could no longer expect letters from Peter or Paul; they would have to rely on what they already had. Thus, whatever inspired writings were available began to be copied and circulated more widely.

The Need for Copies

As time passed, the need for copies of the inspired writings grew. Churches were in need of something suitable for public reading in their worship services. In the past, prophets had addressed the assemblies (1 Corinthians A Growing Need 14:29). But as the prophets passed from the scene, a new source of edification was needed—the writings of "prophets," especially apostles.

The need for copies of authoritative Scriptures increased as false "Scriptures" and other "apocryphal" writings appeared. False teachers began writing books that they hoped would be accepted as Scripture. Frequently, they even forged an apostle's name to a writing in order that it might be accepted. These false Scriptures, called pseudepigrapha, contained much error and false teaching. The church needed a canon by which to measure these false writings.

Other writings appeared that were not intended to deceive but were not Scripture, either. Church leaders wrote letters to churches to provide instruction and encouragement. These letters were not inspired, but they were useful. Often they contained exposition of Scripture, and often they contained opinion. Sometimes, the opinions became a bit fanciful, as Clement's appeal to the legend of the phoenix to prove the resurrection (1 Clement 25). Again, the church needed a canon by which to measure these helpful, but uninspired, writings.

The Development of the Canon

As copies of Scripture and apocryphal writings began to circulate more and more widely, the need increased for an authoritative collection, or canon, of inspired Scripture. Many of the church leaders frequently referred to Scriptural books in their own writings. This indicates the reliability they assigned to Scripture. Occasionally, however, they also referred to apocryphal books. Whether they equated these books with Scripture or merely used them as helpful guides is hard to say. They do, however, help us establish the authorship of many of the canonical books, and thus assure us of their reliability.

The first supposedly "authoritative" collection of canonical books comes from Marcion, a second **Marcion's Canon** century heretic! He rejected many of the **Too Limited** New Testament books, but he accepted none that are now considered noncanonical. His list is useful because he needed to appeal to books of known authority to support his false doctrines. This he did by rejecting many whole books of the New Testament and heavily editing the books he accepted.

The rejection of Marcion's canon is evidence that some kind of "canon" already existed, even though it may not have been in the form of a formal collection. The inspired writings had been accepted from the start and had not lost their authoritative status. Any attempt to deny that authority was bound to raise opposition.

The writings of church leaders continued, revealing much

about the status of the canon. They variously refer to some apocryphal writings as "Scripture," but the books on which there seems to be near universal agreement are those of our present canon, with the exception of some of the general epistles. Some of these writers make specific distinction between Scripture and apocryphal writings.

Toward the end of the second century, the Muratorian Canon was published in Rome. It is a Latin work, but it may have had a Greek source. It includes all of the present canon except Matthew, Mark, Hebrews, James, and 1 and 2 Peter. Luke, however, is called the "third"Gospel, indicating that Matthew and Mark were included originally but have been lost. At least some of the others may also have been lost; it is not possible to say with certainty that these were not part of the original. It contains two apocryphal books, but stipulates that they are for private use and not for public reading.

Muratorian Canon Similar to Present Canon

By the fourth century, the canon was pretty well established. The historian Eusebius gives a list of the books that were disputed by some, but that he affirmed as genuine. The only omission from his list is Revelation. Another church leader, however, wrote a letter in A.D. 367 listing all twenty-seven books as "divine." In A.D. 397, a church council meeting in Carthage declared these twenty-seven books to be canonical.

Clues of Authenticity

With the many writings and teachings circulating, the church needed to know which writings were the Word of God and which were false or mere opinion. As different ones wrestled with the problem of the "canon," they really wrestled with the problem of inspiration.

A major clue in determining which books were inspired was *apostilicity,* that is, having been written by an apostle or a close associate of an apostle. For that reason, Paul's writings were among the first to be collected. Of the twenty-seven New Testament books, twenty-one are attributed to apostles (twenty-two if Hebrews was written by Paul). Mark was a companion of Paul first and later Peter; he wrote under Peter's influence. Luke, who wrote both his Gospel and Acts, was a close associate of Paul—at one point Paul's only companion (2 Timothy 4:11). James and Jude were half brothers to Jesus, and would likely have significant contact with several apostles. James was a prominent elder in the church at Jerusalem while most of the apostles were still in that city. If Hebrews was not written by Paul, it was probably written by one of his companions. Barnabas is frequently suggested. Thus, all the books of the New Testament meet this first criterion.

A second clue in determining the inspiration of the books was *content*. Information about Jesus was highly prized; so the Gospels won reasonably easy acceptance. The content of an inspired writing must also be consistent with other inspired writings. For this reason, many of the false gospels and forged letters were easily spotted as frauds. Others were harder to weed out. Some of the false writings were rejected, not so much for contradictions with Scripture, but for the fanciful incidents related. Some of the apocryphal gospels, for example, pictured Jesus' childhood as a wild time of capricious use of His power. Other writings were hodge-podge collections of true Scripture put together to form other letters to churches. These forgeries were fairly easy to spot.

Apostolicity, Content, Universality, Testimony

A third clue was *universality*. An inspired writing should have universal application and be suitable for public reading in all the churches. This is the point on which some contested the inclusion of the general epistles in the canon. They seemed much too limited—especially 2 and 3 John. But those books had enough recognition from the beginning that they were eventually recognized universally. It is also on this point that many of the apocryphal books were discredited, particularly, for example, those specified for private use only in the Muratorian Canon.

A final major clue was the *testimony* of the church. This

has been hinted at before. From the time the books were written, they were recognized as Scripture. Their validity may later have been questioned, such as in the case of the general epistles, but there were always some who could vouch for the writings' authenticity. Thus, the canon of twenty-seven books came to be established, and that canon is reliable.

Modern Questions

Actually, the canon has still been questioned since the Middle Ages, but no changes have been made. During the Reformation, questions were raised by Reformers and Catholics alike. The conflict within the Catholic Church led to the Council of Trent (1546), which prohibited any further questioning of the canon. Luther developed a split-level canon, with some of the books having more authority (being more inspired?) than others. The epistle of James he called an epistle of "straw," for he found it difficult to harmonize with his understanding of Paul's writings.

Today, questions are raised concerning the authorship of many of the New Testament books. The difference in modern debate and that of earlier times is centered on inspiration. At first, to deny an apostle or a close associate wrote a particular book was to deny inspiration. Thus, authorship was used to determine inspiration. Today, many scholars reject any concept of divine intervention, including inspiration. Having already set inspiration aside, they can do what they like with authorship—it doesn't matter.

Inspiration & Authorship Important

On that basis, they try to determine sources for the writings. This naturally sets the dates of the writings later in order to allow time for circulation and copying. Changing the dates necessarily changes the authors.

However, the present canon was determined on good authority. Most of it had been universally recognized even before the apostles had all died. If these were not inspired writings, the apostles and the church would have exposed them much earlier. We can depend on the New Testament.

9

The Reliability of the Extant Texts

"Build a better mousetrap, and the world will beat a path to your door." Find an original Bible manuscript, and the religious world will beat a path to your door! Such a discovery would truly be a prize, for none has ever been made. In fact, the manuscripts we have are copies of copies—made sometimes hundreds of years later than the originals.

A question, then, can be raised against the reliability of the texts we have (the "extant" texts). How **How Close to the** do we know they are the same as the origi- **Originals?** nal texts we don't have (the "extinct" texts)? Of course, we can't "know" in the sense we can know the things we experience personally. We can only "know" in the sense a jury knows the guilt or innocence of a defendant—by examination of available evidence. And the many who have studied the evidence indicate that with better than 99% certainty, we can believe the extant texts are reliable copies of the originals.

The Old Testament Text

Original manuscripts. The original manuscripts were written in Hebrew, a strange language by our standards, perhaps, for it had no vowels. This was no problem at first, but it became one for copyists as the language changed.

These writings were highly esteemed as sacred from the time of their writing. Therefore, they were treated with special care, unlike any other books in their time. They were carefully guarded, but were not treated as prized "relics." They were much read and studied, which eventually caused them to wear out.

Copies. There were two types of copies made of the Scriptures: official copies, for synagogue use, and unofficial copies, for individual use. The unofficial copies were not done with the same amount of care as the official copies; so they inevitably contained more copying errors. The official copies were made with such precision, however, that the scribes who copied them felt confident enough to destroy the manuscripts from which they copied.

Destroying original documents may seem foreign to our file-bound culture, but it was a way of life for the ancient Jewish scribes. The Talmud (rabbinical laws and commentary on the law of Moses) required that copies of Scripture **Originals Destroyed to Avoid Desecration** be made on animal-skin parchment to replace worn synagogue copies. To avoid desecration, these old copies were to be buried in consecrated ground. There is little doubt that the originals were so buried, just as successive copies and copies of copies were buried.

Although no human is perfect, these scribes approached perfection in their work, bound as they were to the rules in the Talmud. The Talmud required the scribe to look at each letter in the manuscript he was copying before writing it in the new copy. The copy was later checked and errors were corrected. If as many as four errors were found on a single page, the copy was condemned, and a new one had to be made. As further insurance, the scribes counted the verses, words, and even the letters in the manuscripts. They would note sometimes the middle verse or middle letter of a book. If any of these calculations in their copy disagreed with the manuscript being copied, the scribe searched for the error until he found it and corrected it. Sometimes they would make marginal notes or other marks in order to assure accuracy.

The Masoretes were scribes who went beyond the role described above. They were active from around A.D. 750

until A.D. 920. In addition to copying the text and noting the number of words and verses and so on, they developed a system of vowel pointing to clarify the all-consonant text. Hebrew was changing (as all languages do), and the correct pronunciation was being forgotten—especially in certain regions where peculiar dialects had emerged or where Hebrew was becoming a dead language. They added some other notations to aid the reader as well. As a result of their work, the "Masoretic Text" emerged. For many years, this was the best Hebrew text available, and all translations were based on it.

Unfortunately, the oldest manuscripts of the Masoretic Text date back only to around A.D. 900. Most are from A.D. 1100 or later, and no complete text is earlier than that. Although some variation occurs between these manuscripts, there is near perfect agreement.

The Dead Sea Scrolls. It was in 1948 that the world learned of the discovery of Old Testament **Excitement From** manuscripts at Qumran, west of the north **Qumran** end of the Dead Sea. Exploration continued, and fragments of nearly 100 copies of Old Testament books have been found. Every book except Esther has a fragment that was discovered at Qumran and the vicinity.

These manuscripts are important because they date, in some cases, prior to A.D. 100. The discovery made a shambles of some current liberal theories assigning late dates to some of the prophetic books. Thus, it is evidence for inspiration. It is also evidence for the reliability of the text because of the remarkably close agreement with the Masoretic text. One scroll, containing the text of the book of Samuel, is more like the Septuagint than the Masoretic Text, but most of the manuscripts indicate there was very little variation in the text in the thousand years of copying that followed. If the same care was exercised before the Dead Sea Scrolls were made, then we can assume there was very little variation from the originals.

Commentaries and Translations. Ancient commentaries

and translations also speak for the reliability of the extant texts. They are based on copies of the Hebrew that, in some cases, are earlier than the extant copies. The Talmud commented on a text 500 years older than the Masoretic Text, but the agreement is remarkable. The Septuagint, the Greek Old Testament, was translated in 200 B.C. Differences between it and the Hebrew may result from mistaken translation, a difference in the Hebrew version translated, an attempt by the translators to "improve" the text, or some combination of factors. More often, unfortunately, they probably represent attempts to correct the text. It is still useful, however, in helping to determine the original Hebrew in places where the Hebrew text is unintelligible or where there are differences between the Masoretic Text and the Dead Sea Scrolls. There are other less popular ancient translations, including a Syriac and a Latin, which are considerably later than the Septuagint but similarly helpful.

The New Testament

Original manuscripts. The New Testament manuscripts were written in Greek, the world language at that time. These manuscripts were valued by the church similar to the way the Jews valued the Old Testament, but without laws regarding their copying. Thus, the copies that were made were all of an individual nature rather than the scholarly nature of the official copies of the Old Testament. The text was written on papyrus—not a very durable paper for books so heavily used. Thus, the originals and most of the earliest copies have perished.

Only Personal Copies Made of Originals

Copies. Because of the private nature of the copying of the New Testament manuscripts, mistakes more easily slipped into the text—especially when a text was copied by dictation. With the church spreading rapidly, copies of the text were made farther and farther from the originals, with more and more copies between them. And with persecution a way of life until the fourth century, it was not often that Christians could be so bold with a copy as to travel several miles to compare it with earlier copies. Thus, more and more copying mistakes were made part of the text.

This does not mean, however, that the text became so filled with errors that the original message was obscured. The errors are mostly such things as word order or spelling errors. Sometimes this would create a new word, but it never changed a doctrinal point. Other errors might include a scribe's mistaking a marginal comment to be part of the text itself, or making an attempt to "correct" a text.

Such "corrections" may have been just that on occasion, but at times they seem not to have been. Still, all the errors that crept into the text were rather minor.

In the fourth century, Emperor Constantine gave Christianity official recognition. Copying Scripture was no longer a secret enterprise, and comparisons of the texts began to be made. Several discrepancies were found, but the originals had apparently already perished. From the fourth to the eighth centuries, copies began to be "edited," so that the manuscripts began to be more and more similar. Over 90% of the manuscripts now extant come from this period or later; so whatever errors had been introduced in the first four centuries probably remained in the standardized text, depending on how well the editors revised copies to match the originals.

Christianity Approved by Constantine

Copies of the manuscripts were still being made by hand; so a true standard text was not available until Johannes Gutenberg invented printing. However, the texts show a remarkable similarity in those years much like the similarity of Old Testament texts between the Dead Sea Scrolls and the Masoretic Text. The "Gutenberg Bible" (1456) was a Latin translation. After that, several Greek Bibles were also printed, with little variation in the text. That text became known as the "Textus Receptus"—the "received text"— and that text remained the standard until a little more than 100 years ago. In fact, there is still considerable support for the Textus Receptus—the New King James translation (Thomas Nelson, 1980, 1983) has followed it in every

64

instance at which there is any dispute regarding the correct reading.

"Families" of Manuscripts. As copies of the New Testament text were made, and copies of copies, certain "families" of manuscripts began to develop. These seem to center around particular localities, but their age is also a factor. Simply put (perhaps too simply), when a copy was made from the original or earlier copy, the copier often made mistakes. Then, when copies were made from that copy, those mistakes were perpetuated. Thus, all the copies made from that copy are grouped as a family of manuscripts.

It is the concept of families of manuscripts that currently challenges the Textus Receptus. In most cases, the Textus Receptus agrees with the "majority text"; that is, a text based on the majority of extant manuscripts. But it is based on a fairly late family of manuscripts. Earlier manuscripts, though fewer in number, are closer to the original manuscripts and must be considered.

Some of these earlier families have only recently been discovered or identified—within the past 150 years or so. It was B. F. Westcott and F. J. A. Hort who most successfully challenged the Textus Receptus and offered another Greek text in 1881. **Alexandrian the Earliest MS Family** Their text was based on the Alexandrian family—manuscripts coming primarily from around Alexandria and Egypt. This family includes manuscripts and fragments dating as far back as to the second century, including the oldest manuscripts that have yet been found (see chapter 12, "Recent Textual Developments"). The Byzantine family, from the Old Byzantine Empire (Turkey, Greece, Bulgaria, Albania, and Yugoslavia), and the basis of the Textus Receptus, contains no manuscripts from before the fifth century. They do show greater similarity than any other family, but this is probably a result of the standardizing process that occurred after the official recognition of Christianity in the fourth century.

Two other families should also be mentioned. The West-

65

ern family, from the area west of the Mediterranean, also dates back to the second century. Its usefulness is weakened, however, because it contains extensive paraphrases and additions. The Caesarean family was in use in Caesarea. It seems to be a mixture of Alexandrian and Western texts, but it has been spared the major problems of the Western texts.

Commentaries and Translations. As with the Old Testament, ancient commentaries on the Greek text and translations also provide clues to the original. There are many more commentaries on the New Testament than on the Old, but their usefulness, as that of the translations, is limited. So much textual evidence exists that there is less need for this secondary source of evidence. Also, the problems involved in using commentaries and translations is the same as that of the text: it is no easier to determine how reliable a text the commentator or translator was using than it is to determine how reliable a text a copier used.

Similarities in the Text. So far, much has been made of the differences in the text. This is unfortu-

Texts More Alike Than Different nate because the differences are really in the minority. There is amazing similarity in all the texts, and the differences that do exist are minor. Except for spelling and word order, only one word in 1000 is questioned in the Bible texts. No doctrinal point is in jeopardy over a disputed reading. It is much like the study of grammar. So often the discussion of exceptions to the rules overshadows the fact that there are rules. In textual studies, discussion of differences should not overshadow the vast areas of similarity.

Conclusion

There is much evidence to support the Biblical texts now in use. The similarity of manuscripts and the testimony from commentaries and translations have been cited. In addition, differences in the texts are minor. We, therefore, conclude that the extant texts are reliably similar to the originals.

10

Early English Versions

Unless we can turn back the clock to a time when everyone spoke Greek, translations of the Bible will be necessary. Even if we could do that, a translation of the Old Testament would be needed. But time is not turned back, and the problem of translation is here to stay.

Christianity reached Britain during the Roman occupation of that land, in the second century. However, there was no English language at that time. That didn't begin to develop until the fifth century as the Angles and Saxons began influencing the language. Britain had become Angle land, which came to be known later as England. Their language, Anglish, was the foundation for the English language.

Christianity Reaches Britain

Virtually the only translation of the Bible then available was a Latin translation. The Roman Church felt that only the clergy should be permitted to read Scripture, for the common people might misunderstand and misapply it. However, the people's love for the Word of God prompted paraphrases to appear. As early as A.D. 670, a poet named Caedman was paraphrasing parts of the Bible—perhaps from memory of Biblical narratives—in verse form in the Old English language.

Fortunately, not all of the Roman clergy regarded the common people's intelligence lightly. Some of the earliest English translations of the Scripture (from the Latin) were made by bishops, priests, and monks. Around A.D. 700, the bishop of Sherborne, Aldhelm, translated the book of Psalms. A monk named Bede, an outstanding scholar, translated portions of the New Testament into English. He is said to have finished translating the book of John on his deathbed in 735. A priest named Aldred has left his legacy by writing a word-for-word translation of the Latin between the lines of the Latin manuscript of the bishop of Lindisfarne—thus producing an interlinear translation. This translation, dated around 950, is the earliest English translation of the Gospels. Later in that century, an abbot named Aelfric translated parts of the Old Testament from Genesis through Judges.

Thus, the English people were getting portions of Scripture in their own language. Several other translations were also being made, but they were all incomplete. The people remained dependent on the public reading of Scripture and on sermons from their priests, who knew Latin, for their understanding of God's Word.

Wycliffe

It was not until 1382 that English-speaking people had a complete Bible in their own language. Then, **First English Bible** a complete English translation of the Latin Bible was written. It was called the Wycliffe Bible after John Wycliffe, who didn't necessarily translate the Bible himself, but was instrumental in getting the job done. We don't know who actually did the translating, except that a monk named Nicholas de Hereford did much of the Old Testament. Wycliffe may also have done some of the translating. A revision of the Wycliffe Bible appeared in 1388, four years after Wycliffe's death. This Bible was done by Wycliffe's secretary, John Purvey. This Bible was a less literal, more natural translation and was more popular with the people.

The Wycliffe Bible, especially the second edition, had a wide influence both immediately and over the years. This is a bit remarkable under the circumstances. First, it was written more than sixty years before the invention of printing. Thus, every copy had to be made by hand, a slow, arduous task. Yet the task was taken in hand many times, and the

Word of God spread. About 170 copies of the Wycliffe Bible are still in existence. Second, the Roman Church had declared Wycliffe a heretic.

Although Wycliffe died 133 years before Luther posted his ninety-five theses (the act usually considered the beginning of the Reformation), Wycliffe was a Reformer much like Luther. He opposed the authority of the pope and **Pre-Reformation Reformer** of canon law. He opposed the power of the church in government and the dishonest "sale" of official positions. He opposed the practices of corrupt priests, whose blessings could be "bought" for a price. He upheld the rights of the common people to know and study the Bible for themselves.

All this brought Wycliffe and his followers into confrontation with the church authorities. When Wycliffe's Bible was translated, one church official said Wycliffe had "completed his iniquity," and the translation was condemned. Nicholas was summoned to London and excommunicated. Wycliffe himself was denounced and his followers called "Lollards," which means "mutterers." Apparently they were memorizing and reciting Scriptures, a practice the church officials found offensive.

In spite of the opposition, Wycliffe's movement caught on. Even after his death, his ideals were championed, even in other countries. One famous follower of Wycliffe, John Huss, was burned at the stake in 1415. In 1428, Wycliffe's remains were dug up and burned. Laws were passed outlawing the possession of English Scriptures. Those caught with Bibles were burned at the stake, often with their Bibles tied around their necks. At other times, great searches were made for Bibles, which were collected and burned. But the movement was not crushed. People continued to have access to the Word of God.

Tyndale

In the years after Wycliffe's Bible was written, the world was shaken by a "revival of learning," and the church was shaken by Luther and the Reformation. Scriptures were being translated in German, French, and Italian. Printing was invented, and Erasmus published his Greek text of the New Testament (basically the same as the Textus Receptus). But in England, no new translations appeared for nearly 150 years.

William Tyndale, a noted scholar of Oxford and Cambridge, began at an early age to yearn for a new and better English Bible. He tried to get help from the church in 1523 to make his dream a reality, but the church continued its anti-Bible policy. Instead of help, he got hindrance, and in 1524, he was forced to leave England to escape persecution and to pursue his dream.

In 1525, Tyndale published an English New Testament, translated from the Greek text instead of the

Tyndale's Translation Reaches England

Latin translation. Copies were smuggled into England, where the bishop of London attempted to buy all the copies in order to burn them. His plan backfired, however, because it financed Tyndale's first revisions of his New Testament as well as his translation of the Old Testament. This translation was based on the Hebrew text, with help from the Latin and earlier English translations.

In 1535, Tyndale was arrested. He was strangled and burned at the stake one year later. His dying prayer was that the eyes of the king of England be opened. Actually, the prayer was beginning to be answered even before he prayed it. Henry VIII had broken with the Roman Church in 1534, and discussion was already taking place in England about allowing an English translation. (Such a move would clearly indicate the break with Rome.) Queen Anne Boleyn even possessed a copy of Tyndale's New Testament.

Coverdale

Miles Coverdale was an English priest, somewhat older than Tyndale. He was an avid Bible student, and desired to have the Bible published in English. Although the idea did not receive "official" endorsement from the English government, it seems to have been encouraged by Secretary of State Thomas Cromwell.

In 1535, the Coverdale Bible was published. The Old Testament from Genesis through 2 Chronicles and the New Testament were basically the work of Tyndale. Coverdale made some slight revisions based on the Latin Vulgate and Luther's German translation. Coverdale himself translated the rest of the Old Testament, but he used the Latin rather than the Hebrew text.

Thus, a complete English Bible was in print one year before Tyndale's death, and much of it was his own work. This fact was not common knowledge, however, probably because so much opposition had been raised against Tyndale that his contribution could not be admitted. The Bible carried a dedication to King Henry VIII, and the king made no attempt to destroy it. Finally, the English people had ready access to the Word of God.

Tyndale's Work Kept Secret

Other Versions

In 1537, one year after Tyndale's death, the martyr's prayer was answered. King Henry VIII issued a license for the publication of a new English Bible, called the *Matthew's Bible* because the name Thomas Matthew is given on the dedication page. The name is an alias for the editor, John Rogers. Rogers had been with Tyndale in the last years of Tyndale's life, and had possession of the last of Tyndale's unpublished translations.

Rogers was considered a heretic, as was Tyndale; so his real name could not be used. His Bible was a revision of the Coverdale Bible, with the Tyndale manuscripts added. About two thirds of the work is actually Tyndale's. In 1555, Rogers returned to England, but he was not as well received as his Bible. He was arrested and burned at the stake.

In 1539, Miles Coverdale published the *Great Bible*. This was a revision of the Matthew's Bible intended for use in the churches. It was ordered by Thomas Cromwell, this time with the official sanction of the king. It was printed in a larger size than previous Bibles (thus, the "Great" Bible) and on better paper, and lacked the biased notes of the Matthew's Bible. A copy was placed in each church so that people could come and read it. Thus, even those who could not afford private copies of the Bible had easy access to the Word of God. This Bible was in print for thirty years.

Also in 1539, Richard Taverner published a revision of the Matthew's Bible. *Taverner's Bible* was the first English Bible printed in London, but it was not as popular as other versions and was only reprinted once.

Between 1539 and 1560, the attitude toward Bible trans-lations swung like a pendulum. In 1543, **More Opposition** Henry VIII, who had sanctioned the Great **to Bibles** Bible, turned against English Bibles. His anti-Catholic policies had got Cromwell be-headed, and he feared for his own life as well. Bibles were destroyed and Bible reading was outlawed—both in public and in the homes—to placate the Catholics. Edward VI reversed his father's decrees in 1547, but Mary Tudor switched things back in 1553. In her attempt to make England Catholic again, she took the traditional Catholic stance. (It was she who had Rogers executed.) Elizabeth, in 1558, returned the Bible to English churches.

In 1560, the *Geneva Bible* was published. This was an English Bible published in Geneva (and later in England) by scholars who had fled England under the reign of "Bloody Mary." This Bible included many notes opposing the pope and supporting Calvin's theology. It was the first to use the chapter and verse arrangement (Wycliffe had divided the Bible into chapters—but not verses) and to italicize words not actually found in the Greek and Hebrew.

The *Bishops' Bible* was printed in 1568. The Great Bible had been seen as inferior to the Geneva Bible, but the latter Bible's marginal notes were seen as too objectionable for a church Bible. Thus, nine English bishops, led by Matthew Parker of Canterbury, revised the Great Bible for use in the churches. It was better than the Great Bible, but not as good as the Geneva Bible, which remained very popular. The

Bishops' Bible remained the official version of the churches, however, until 1611, when the *King James Version* appeared.

During the reign of Elizabeth, a large number in England who were loyal Catholics fled to France, which was still Catholic. Some of them, however, were beginning to desire to read the Bible for themselves. For this, they had to use translations the Roman Church had banned as heretical. Eventually, even the Roman Church was forced to soften its position on Bible translations.

In 1582, a Catholic translation of the New Testament was made at Rheims, France. In 1610, the Old Testament was completed at Douay. This **A Catholic Bible** Bible became known as the *Douay-Rheims* **Published** *Version,* or simply the Douay Version. It was translated from the Latin Vulgate, although the Greek and Hebrew were occasionally consulted. Although it was inferior to other English Bibles, and especially to the King James, which appeared the next year, the English Catholics finally had a Bible they could read for themselves with the sanction of the church.

Today, with the Bible so accessible in several excellent versions, it is hard to imagine the great pain and effort it took to get the Bible into the English language. The names of Wycliffe and Tyndale ought not to be forgotten, for the debt we owe them is immense. And should political turmoil ever arise so that the Bible is again suppressed, their example ought to be our guide as we value the Word of God above our own lives.

11

The King James Version

No other English Bible has had more impact on English speaking people than the King James Version (also called the Authorized Version). First produced in 1611, it has been the favorite version for over 350 years. It not only provided an excellent translation of the available texts, but is unmatched in literary quality.

Background History

The religious situation in England during the reign of Elizabeth was not one of unity. Not only was there division between the Church of England (Anglican) and the Roman Catholic Church, but within the Anglican Church there was also division. Those who wanted more reforms in the church were called Puritans, and some of them began to leave the Anglican Church and form independent churches.

Division in the Anglican Church

The Anglican Church was still tied to the government, however. In 1593 these radical Puritans were branded as traitors. They were ordered either to worship in the Anglican Church or to leave England. Although some of them did leave, most of the Puritans remained with the Anglican Church to work for reforms from within. Their main hope was that the successor to the aging Elizabeth would be more favorable to their views.

In 1603, King James VI of Scotland became King James I of England. Immediately the Puritans presented a petition signed by nearly 1000 Puritan clergymen—one tenth of all the Anglican clergy. King James did not take the petition lightly. He called for a conference to address the differences between the Anglican bishops and the Puritans. The conference convened in Hampton Court in January of 1604. Although not many of the differences were resolved, the conference was important in that a new translation of the Scriptures was proposed.

At that time, two Bibles were especially popular in England. The Puritans favored the Geneva Bible. The bishops opposed that translation, mainly for its marginal notes. James himself voiced opposition to the Geneva Bible for the same reason. The official Bible of the Anglican Church was the Bishops' Bible. This translation was better than the version it replaced—the Great Bible—but was still inferior to the Geneva translation.

Opposition to Current Translations

The new translation that was proposed would have no marginal notes. This would keep the Bible from becoming sectarian. It was also to be as faithful as possible to the original Hebrew and Greek. It was not to be a translation of the Latin as many previous Bibles had been. And it would be translated by both Puritan and traditional Anglican university scholars. This would prevent biased translating on points where these two groups disagreed. The work would be reviewed by the bishops, the Privy Council, and finally by the king himself. It was to be the only Bible read in the Church of England—hence, the name, the Authorized Version.

The Translation

Fifty-four scholars were selected for the translation, and forty-seven of them actually participated. These were divided into six groups, each of which was assigned a different portion of Scripture. Each man on the team would translate all of the assigned Scripture; then the whole group would compare and refine their results. After that, their work would be sent to the other groups, who would make suggestions for revision. When all the groups had finished their work, two men from each group formed a committe of twelve to make further revisions. It was this committee that acted on the suggestions made earlier by the groups. Their work was then reviewed by the bishops, the Privy Council, and the king.

The translators had more resources available to them than those of any previous version. They **Superior Resources Available** used all four of the Hebrew versions of the Old Testament then available. All of these were variations of the Masoretic Text, with probably very little difference among them. For the New Testament, they used the Textus Receptus as revised by Beza (John Calvin's associate). In addition, they made use of several Latin, English, and other versions.

The translators were very careful about their work. They rushed nothing, but worked very deliberately. Each one was concerned with producing a faithful English rendering of the Word of God. Not one of them was paid, a fact that speaks highly of their commitment. It took them six years to deliver their translation to the printer, who took an additional nine months to complete the first printing. Thus, it was 1611 when the King James Bible finally became available to the public. It carried a dedication to the king, but no official action was ever taken by James to "authorize" this version.

Revisions

Although many people today claim to use the 1611 King James Version, such is not the case. English has changed considerably since then, and the modern reader would have some difficulty understanding 1611 English. The spelling of several words was not even standardized for some years to come.

Between 1611 and 1616 several small revisions were made in the King James Bible. Printer's errors (such as the omission of *not* from the seventh commandment) were corrected as well as small errors made by the translators and editors themselves. Major revisions—involving the actual text—were made in 1629 and 1638. These revisions were intended to reflect the actual intentions of the original translators, not to change their work. In 1762 and 1769, further revisions were made at Cambridge and Oxford. The King James Bibles in use today are the result of these revisions on the 1611 translation.

Literature

In the field of literature, no English Bible can match the King James Version. It has been quoted by authors and poets for centuries. Even people who make no claim to Christianity often can quote phrases and "mottos" from the King James Bible, sometimes without even realizing it. It has a style and rhythm found in the works of such great writers as Shakespeare and Milton. Schools that have banned Bible study or other religious activities from their halls have yet offered classes in the Bible as "literature."

Unequalled as Literature

It is, no doubt, this feature that has allowed the King James Version to remain so popular for so many years. Originally, its language was fairly common, although it was even in 1611 recognized as quality writing. Still, it took nearly fifty years to establish itself as the most popular Bible. But the enduring nature of its language has enabled it to maintain that position ever since. No one revises Shakespeare; his classic works stand on their own. And no one, for the sake of literature, revises the King James Bible.

Every Christian who appreciates fine literature should familiarize himself with the King James Bible. Not only will its majestic tones thrill the heart, but the study of other literature will be enhanced as well. Seldom does an author cite book, chapter, and verse when quoting or alluding to Scripture (except in theological studies). The real significance of these references is lost if the reader does not recognize them as Scripture.

But not everyone appreciates literature. Reading for pleasure is practically a dying art. Electronic media have replaced reading to a very large extent. Young people are graduating from high schools barely able to read even simple things. So reading seventeenth century English is not particularly popular. Although Shakespeare is definitely classic literature, he is seldom on the top ten best seller list. And even though the King James Bible is also classic literature, many people simply cannot understand it, or do not wish to try.

The Bible was never written to be heralded as great literature. The purpose of the Bible is to communicate the will of God to man. The King James Bible did that better than any other version in 1611 and for many years after. It continues to communicate that will beautifully to those who are comfortable with its style and vocabulary. But for most people—especially those who have not grown up in the church—a more contemporary version is needed.

The Text

The problem of people's being unable to understand King James English is not the only problem in today's use of the King James Version. Another problem is the text itself. The finest texts available in 1611 were used by King James' translators. But textual developments since then have demonstrated certain weaknesses in that text. This problem will be considered in the next chapter.

Before discussing the problem of the text, however, a word of caution is in order. The differences **Textual** between the text of the King James Version **Variations Slight** and that of more recent Bibles are minor. The way of salvation and the will of God are clearly revealed in the King James Version if the reader is able to understand its antique language.

The King James Version remains the most popular English Bible ever. Its classic language, though difficult for some to understand today, has been communicating the will of God for over three and a half centuries. Its majestic style has been quoted, paraphrased, and imitiated like no other. Its influence in Christian hymns is unmistakable. Although recent textual developments have shown some weaknesses, the King James Version will likely remain the most popular English translation for many years to come.

12

Recent Textual Developments

The King James Version of the Bible was based on the best Greek and Hebrew texts available. This contributed immeasurably to its worth, for most English Bibles had been translated from a Latin translation. Thus, the King James took English readers a full step closer to the original message.

But that was over 350 years ago. Archeology has contributed much to Biblical studies since that time. And textual criticism has made some significant advances since then as well. These contributions are the subject of the present chapter.

Contributions of Archeology & Textual Criticism

The King James Bible was based on the Masoretic Text of the Old Testament (which dates back to about A.D. 900) and the Textus Receptus of the New Testament (which dates back to A.D. 1515). It was in consideration of the New Testament text that significant developments first appeared, for the evidence is much more plentiful for it than for the Old.

Weaknesses in the Textus Receptus

The King James Version of the New Testament was based on Beza's edition of the Textus Receptus. This text was assembled in the city of Basel in 1515 by a scholar named Erasmus. Cardinal Ximenes of Spain was having another Greek text printed at the same time. This text was part of a Bible called the Complutensium Polyglot (Complutensium for the city in which it was published; Polyglot for "many tongues" or "many languages"—it included Greek, Hebrew, and Latin).

Erasmus was a Reformer and probably wanted to publish a text ahead of the Catholic version. Thus, he hastily put it together from incomplete manuscripts available in his own city of Basel. Only one was not of the standardized form resulting from work done in the fourth century. This he used sparingly. None of his manuscripts contained the last six verses of Revelation; so he translated those verses into Greek from the Latin. His text was published in 1516, four years ahead of the Complutensium Polyglot.

Textus Receptus Assembled Hastily

Between 1546 and 1551, Robert Estienne, known as Stephanus, published four editions of Erasmus' text. He introduced the first critical apparatus in a Greek text—notes indicating different manuscript readings as well as differences in the Complutensium Polyglot. Beza's work included nine editions of this text, done between 1565 and 1604. The term *Textus Receptus* (*"received text"*) did not come until 1633 in a preface to a later-published edition. Technically speaking, the Textus Receptus was that later edition, but it varied little from the texts of Erasmus and Stephanus.

During the first two centuries following the publication of the King James Bible, scholars studied more and more manuscripts. Differences were noted in several of them from the reading of the Textus Receptus. Some scholars began to suggest changes in the text, but they were little heeded. Some were even attacked for undermining the Scriptures.

One of the most important developments from this period was the beginning to view manuscripts in "families." Although the majority of manuscripts still support the Textus Receptus, number alone does not establish the best reading. A more important consideration is the number of "families" of texts that are represented.

Let us suppose that a particular passage has twenty manuscripts behind it, and three different readings. Reading A is supported by twelve manuscripts, reading B by seven, and reading C by one. Reading C is the most unlikely choice because it is unique, although if its manuscript were the earliest one available, it would be given more weight. Suppose that all the manuscripts supporting reading A could be traced to a common source—all the other manuscripts are copies of that source or copies of such copies. Thus, only one family is represented. If reading B demonstrates two or more independent sources, or "families," then it is more likely the better reading, especially if at least one of the sources is an early one.

In the nineteenth century, textual criticism was becoming an important study. One critic, Tischendorf, was so thorough in the textual apparatus to his Greek text that it remains an invaluable source for modern textual critics.

Westcott and Hort

The work of two scholars from Cambridge University, B. F. Westcott and F. J. A. Hort, remains the most outstanding in the conflict with the Textus Receptus. Their Greek text was published in 1881 and 1882, along with a comprehensive work explaining the principles by which they worked. The English Revised Version of the New Testament, also published in 1881, used the Greek text of Westcott and Hort, who were among the translators. This gave that text additional credibility. Nearly all current translations follow a text much like that of Westcott and Hort.

Westcott and Hort believed they recognized four different families of manuscripts. One family, which they called the *neutral* text, was based on two important codex manuscripts, Vaticanus and Sinaiticus. Sinaiticus is the earliest complete New Testament text. Vaticanus, though somewhat later in origin, is believed to be more true to the original, but it is not a complete text. These manuscripts were not available to the King James translators. Although Vaticanus was known to be in the Vatican Library as early as 1448, no one was permitted to study it until 1867, when

Vaticanus & Sinaiticus

Tischendorf was permitted to study and publish its text. Sinaiticus was not discovered until 1844. It was also Tischendorf who discovered this manuscript, in the monastery of St. Catherine in the Sinai peninsula.

The other families, by Westcott and Hort's evaluation, were the Alexandrian, the Western, and the Syrian. Today, Vaticanus and Sinaiticus are considered Alexandrian texts. Although they are highly reliable, they probably are not as near-original as Westcott and Hort believed. Many scholars will reject the reading of these manuscripts on certain passages when abundant evidence is available, but Westcott and Hort had taken their agreement as absolute.

Other Developments

In addition to the codex manuscripts, Vaticanus and Sinaiticus, several early papyrus manuscripts have also been discovered since 1895. These have been found in Egypt and support the Alexandrian text. These include the very early fragment of John, mentioned earlier, called the John Rylands fragment. It is one of the "Bodmer papyri." In 1930 and 1931, the "Chester Beatty papyri" came to light. These two sets of papyrus manuscripts added significantly to textual criticism because they are the earliest extant manuscripts, dating from the second through the fourth centuries, plus one from the seventh century.

Bodmer & Chester Beatty Payri

Other Greek texts have also been assembled since Westcott and Hort's. One is the Nestle's text, which combines the work of Westcott and Hort with that of Tischendorf and Weiss. Another, the United Bible Society text, has been in publication since 1966. It was edited by Kurt Aland, Matthew Black, Carlo Martin, Bruce Metzger, and Alan Wikgren. These two are very similar and are sometimes considered together, as they both rely primarily on the Alexandrian texts. The New American Standard Bible is based on the Nestle text. The New International Version follows a combination of the Nestle and United Bible Society texts. These would be good versions for the English reader to compare with the King James Version to see textual differences from the Textus Receptus. The New King James Version includes footnotes that make such comparisons even easier.

The Dead Sea Scrolls

The discovery of the Dead Sea Scrolls at Qumran in 1947 and since has been the most important development in Old Testament textual study. **Most Important** The scrolls moved the modern reader 1000 **OT Development** years closer to the original manuscripts. Although several small differences have been noticed, the agreement with the previously earliest texts is amazing.

More differences from the Masoretic Text have been noticed in the Dead Sea Scrolls representing the book of Samuel than for any other book. The recently discovered manuscripts agree more closely with the Septuagint than with the Masoretic Text. Interestingly, Samuel is considered by some to be the least well preserved book in all of the Masoretic Text. Perhaps the Dead Sea Scrolls will provide a better reading for this book than has ever been available.

Although the first discovery at Qumran was forty years ago, not all the evidence is in. It will take many more years of diligent study to mine all the worth out of the Dead Sea Scrolls. New developments could come at any time.

Language Studies

Advances in the study of languages has also been important to the translating of the Bible. We have noted the value of ancient versions of the Bible in textual studies. But these versions are only helpful if they, too, can be translated. Advances in language studies have increased the value of these versions.

Such advances have helped in other ways, too. Ancient languages that are similar to the Hebrew language have been especially helpful in translating the Old Testament. There does not need to be a version of the Old Testament in one of these languages for the language itself to assist the

Bible translator. Similarities in the languages can be evaluated and conclusions can be drawn even without the same text being in both languages. The Arabic, Akkadian, and Ugaritic languages have all added to our knowledge of Hebrew, and have, thus, assisted in the translation of the Old Testament. And most of these advances have come since the translation of the King James Bible.

New Translations

Bible scholars have been trying to incorporate the newer

Incorporating Textual Developments

textual developments into new revised translations for centuries. The King James Version was produced with the same idea in mind, and a wealth of other translations have appeared since. Their purpose, usually, is more than to update the language. These versions have attempted to take the English reader even closer to the original Word of God.

The English Revised Version (or simply the Revised Version) appeared in 1881. In 1901, the American committee that had been involved in that translation produced the American Standard Version. This version incorporated readings that the American committee had favored, but which had not been accepted in the English version.

In 1952, the Revised Standard Version appeared, a theologically liberal revision of the American Standard Version. In 1971, another revision of this work was completed—the New American Standard Bible. This is a much more conservative work and is actually more of a new translation than a revision. In 1978, the New International Version was completed. Its freer translation produced a smoother English that has been very well received.

In 1982, the New King James Version was completed. This translation reflects the thinking that the Textus Receptus, or the Byzantine text, is actually the best New Testament text, in spite of recent discoveries. It is a new revision of the King James Version, being much easier to read and understand than the King James.

Conclusion

Literally hundreds of manuscripts and fragments of manuscripts have been discovered since the production of the King James Bible. Many of these are much older than any of the texts available in 1611.

Although there is some debate on which texts more accurately reflect the original manuscripts, most scholars favor the more recently discovered manuscripts. The newer translations, except for the New King James Version, reflect that belief. **Recent Discoveries Favored** This belief has made some changes in the text necessary, and it is sometimes difficult to follow along in these versions with a reader who is reading the King James. But the basic message is unchanged.

The recent discoveries have not altered the text nearly as much as they have confirmed it. They have given evidence of inspiration and have thwarted liberal theories that had proposed a different origin for the Bible. The textual changes—though significant in number—have not been radical in content. No doctrinal point has been changed. No "new gospel" has been preached. It's still the same old story of God's grace and love.

13

An Evaluation of Some Current Translations*

The choice of a Bible translation is important. Examples will be given here as to how a few of the more important translations can be assessed. Each Bible reader must do this for himself. The following judgments are only one person's opinion. Each person is responsible for doing his own reading and drawing his own conclusions. These same criteria can and should be used on other translations as well.

The author is reluctant simply to give labels of *excellent, good, fair,* and *poor* in such categories as

Hard to Attach Labels
accuracy, beauty, and *clarity,* but it is impossible to set down a more detailed assessment in as short a study as this. Rather than conclude the study with no concrete results, it seems best to give frank conclusions. The reader is not asked to agree with the estimates, but to "walk circumspectly" in his own selection of a Bible translation.

One may question the wisdom of going any further with an estimate if a translation does not measure up in the area of accuracy. After all, if the work does not faithfully represent the Word of God, of what value is beauty or clarity in translation? Hopefully, many readers share and admire that feeling. Many, however, have already used different translations of the Bible and drawn their own conclusions

*Adapted from "Making a Judgment," *Selecting a Translation of the Bible,* by Lewis A. Foster, © 1978, 1983, The STANDARD PUBLISHING Company, Cincinnati, Ohio.

86

in the areas of beauty and clarity, but have not stopped to think about accuracy. To put accuracy in proper perspective, it is well to recognize the other categories in an independent way, but not to allow them first place in the criteria. Then, too, each of the translations under consideration here shows some measure of accuracy. The Lord can be known through truths expressed in each of them; the way of salvation can be learned.

The King James Version (1611)

ACCURACY: Good. As a literal translation, its observance of details helps the rating of accuracy.
The fact that earlier manuscripts have been **Faithful to** discovered since 1611 does not render the **the Text** KJV unsatisfactory, since the differences are not that great and the KJV is extremely faithful to the text then available. Italics inform the reader when words are added in the English that do not have an equivalent in the Hebrew or Greek. One passage, 1 John 5:7, is a later Latin addition that should not be included in the text.

BEAUTY: Excellent. Although beauty in language is somewhat dependent upon each individual's judgment, one must recognize the time-tested preference for the majestic expression and cadence of this translation.

CLARITY: Often unsatisfactory. Not only are many words obsolete or now different in meaning, but some passages are unnecessarily obscured; for example, 2 Corinthians 10:15, 16.

The New American Standard Bible (1971)

ACCURACY: Excellent. A twofold purpose is expressed in the foreword: "to adhere as closely as possible to the original languages of the Holy Scriptures and to make the translation in a fluent and readable style according to the current English usage." The overall accuracy of the translation is high because of the balance of closeness to the original and good expression in the English to convey the true meaning of the original.

BEAUTY: Fair. Of necessity, a literal translation cannot achieve the literary naturalness that a free translation can. The NASB makes clear the intention to give careful distinction in translating the tenses of the Greek verbs. This in itself results in an unnatural straining at the tenses in the English. The overall dignity of the work compensates somewhat for the staid results in reaching for the literal.

CLARITY: Good. It is much more clear than the King James Version, but remaining literal still restrains the translator from adding words to clarify a passage further.

The Revised Standard Version (1952)

ACCURACY: Deficient in vital areas. The translators depart from the Hebrew text (O.T.) to make **Deficient in Vital** conjectural renderings without inserting any **Areas** note. F. F. Bruce (*The English Bible: A History of Translation* [1970], p. 194) concluded that the RSV has "blurred some of the finer distinctions in New Testament wording which, while they are of little importance to the general reader, have some significance for those who are concerned with the more accurate interpretation of the text."

BEAUTY: Fair. Once again it is emphasized that this is a subjective judgment. Compared with the trite language of some modern speech, the RSV is beautiful. The translators conscientously attempted to preserve a dignity making this version suitable for pulpit reading. But even if one does not choose to use the King James Version as a standard for beauty, the RSV suffers by restricting itself as a revision of the King James Version, and the result is not natural enough to establish its own style of beauty.

CLARITY: Good. The translators' primary goal was to

88

make the translation understandable, and they reached a measure of success in this area. Even here there is room for improvement. What is a *refractory* slave (Titus 2:9)? Does *ablutions* (Hebrews 6:2) make *baptisms* (KJV) more understandable? *Elemental spirits* (Galatians 4:3) is no improvement over *elements of the world* (KJV) and looks in the wrong direction for meaning.

The Good News Bible (1976)

ACCURACY: Fair. Although the free translation will not show detailed accuracy, the message comprehension must be improved to justify its moving from the literal. Often this is not the case in the GNB. For example, *Before the world was created* (John 1:1) is used to paraphrase *In the beginning,* but it is unnecessary. Deep passages are like unopened packages. John chose to hand the reader an unopened package—*In the beginning,* but the translator interjects himself and says, "Here, let me open the package for you. What John means to say is 'the beginning of the world.' " This is not a service to the reader but simply deprives him of the joy of opening the package himself as he contemplates how the Word is prior to all beginnings. In like manner, the translator mars the ultimate in simplicity and profundity, *and the Word was God,* by rendering it *and he was the same as God.* The translator has only succeeded in making fuzzy what is sharp in the Greek. While the passage is difficult to understand, it does not help to make it shallow by introducing a translation pointing to God-like instead of God. The word order and the absence of the article have their significance in the Greek, but they still point to an accurate English as simple and startling as the Greek, *and the Word was God.*

Bratcher, the translator, is more successful than most in presenting a fresh, new, free translation and at the same time preserving the true thrust of the text. Frequently a person will react to a rendering and then check on it, only to find that the idea is right there in the original. But the in-

Opens the Package

stances of welcome enlightenment cannot always compensate for the shortcomings.

BEAUTY: Fair. The literary quality is judged differently by different people. The style is simple and direct, but one feels he is on a choppy sea rather than on a swift flowing stream. It is marred by such unnecessary expressions as "May you and your money go to hell . . ." (Acts 8:20).

The present format of the GNB uses the double column to the page. This is a disadvantage in reading but makes the book a convenient size.

One of the distinguishing characteristics of the Good News Bible is that the text is illustrated with line drawings by Mlle. Anne Vallotton. At first these caricatures seem out of place, but then interest in them grows. One wonders whether the style and application are a part of the authentic Bible message.

CLARITY: Good. The work was designed to meet the needs of non-Christian readers as well as **Instructive** Christians, for those who have limited for- **Clarity for All** mal education, and for those who have learned English as a second language. With these especially in mind, the translation comes through with a clarity for all and in an instructive way.

The Living Bible (1971)

ACCURACY: Poor. It would be unfair to require of a paraphrase the same formal-detail accuracy expected of a translation. On the other hand, the paraphrase must present such clarity and impact of the authentic message to justify departing from the wording and form of the original. In this area, The Living Bible is deficient. Innovations appear without helping the message or the proper impact. The Psalms and Proverbs lack something when written in prose instead of the poetic form. A "P.S." tacked on to Paul's letter to the Philippians leaves a false impression. The prologue to Luke's Gospel in this paraphrase sounds as though Luke's

90

work were simply rechecking previous accounts without going to the early disciples and eyewitnesses himself (compare with Luke 1:1-4, NASB). Whether a work is a translation or a paraphrase, it must be faithful to the meaning, intent, and impact of the original.

BEAUTY: Fair. If beauty meant readability, then the Living Bible would rank high. Literally millions have thrilled to its words. Some, however, comparing it with the beauty of the King James Version, consciously or unconsciously, consider it inferior. But this is not a fair comparison. The English literary quality of the King James Version may be above the Greek literary quality of the New Testament; the best translation would be on the same level. However, the English literary quality of the Living Bible seems below the literary level of New Testament Greek.

Highly Readable

CLARITY: Good. If clarity were the only criterion, the Living Bible would be outstanding. Its purpose, as stated in the preface, "is to say as exactly as possible what the writers of the Scripture meant, and to say it simply, expanding where necessary for a clear understanding by the modern reader." This is the worthy goal held before Kenneth Taylor, the corps of Greek and Hebrew experts who checked for content, and the English critics who made suggestions for style. They have succeeded in presenting a clear, fast-moving narrative that has drawn the interest of many. It has been effective in evangelizing the nonbeliever. It has spoken to a generation of youth. But the worth of its clarity is diluted just to that degree to which it does not do what it set out to do—"to say as exactly as possible what the writers of the Scripture meant." All too often the idea in the paraphrased passage is not the idea of the Scripture.

The New International Version (1978)
ACCURACY: Good. Although this is a free translation, it attempts to acknowledge each Hebrew or Greek word in

some way—if not by a word in the English, then at least by word order, punctuation, or some device. It is contemporary in selection of words, and emulates the mood as well as the message of a passage. In some ways, it is closer to the Greek than most former translations; for example, in 1 Timothy 3:16, for "inspired of God" the NIV has "all Scripture is God-breathed."

BEAUTY: Good. The NIV combines a dignity suitable for use in public worship with a freshness of expression. This is not the beauty of the King James Version, but it has a contemporary beauty without being trite. Many editions are available, both single and double-column; the format is pleasing and has frequent paragraphs. Verse designations are small and footnotes are kept to a minimum in order not to slow the progress of the reader.

Dignity & Freshness

CLARITY: Excellent. This version has been refined through a four-tiered committee approach, resulting in more checking and cross-checking than the known procedure of any other translation work. The product gives evidence of this scrutiny. The language is contemporary, and the meaning is clear. But complete consistency is never accomplished. Some difficult or easily misunderstood words are rendered in a newer way: *Propitiation,* Romans 3:25, becomes *sacrifice of atonement.* (Is this any clearer?) In other places, however, difficult words are left in the text: *phylacteries* (Matthew 23:5) and *tetrarch* (Luke 9:7). Absolute consistency need not be demanded, but in these instances, it may have been wiser to leave the former unchanged in the text and explained by a footnote, and the latter changed in the text.

The New King James Version (1982)
ACCURACY: Good. Endangering its accuracy is the textual basis for the work. In the body of the translation, it follows the *Textus Receptus* of the 1611 King James even if

.

the Majority Text and the Nestle/United Bible Text both depart from it. For examples of this, see 1 John 5:7, 8 and Luke 18:36. This means that no possibility is allowed for a single change based upon the findings in the thousands of manuscripts that have come to light since the seventeenth-century King James translation was made.

In spite of this negative feature, the accuracy is considered good in general, because:

1) Even though a great number of differences do exist between the manuscripts grouped as the Majority Text and those grouped as the Nestle/United Bible Societies' Text, there are relatively few examples of crucial changes involved in the decisions.

2) These points of difference are noted in the footnotes of the NKJV.

3) The NKJV keeps close to the Greek text and faithful to the context of meaning in its translation methods. Examples of changes for greater accuracy: dropping the word "unknown" from the description of the tongues referred to in 1 Corinthians 14:2ff; rendering "Passover" instead of "Easter" in Acts 12:4.

BEAUTY: Good. It is difficult to estimate how the beauty of this translation will be judged after a passage of time. It seems to have retained much **Combines Old &** of the cadence and majesty of the 1611 **New Quality** King James, but it may have lost some of its older charm through the very deleting of the archaisms. Furthermore, the fact that it is a literal translation of necessity hinders the natural flow of expression in the English. Nevertheless, this revision is not crude or patchy. It introduces a dignity and forceful grandeur of its own. For example, read 1 Corinthians 13:1ff. It sounds familiar, but note some changes that are improvements but do not mar the beauty: instead of "tinkling cymbal" (not characteristic of cymbals), the NKJV has "clanging cymbal"; instead of "charity vaunteth not itself," the wording is changed to "love does not parade itself."

CLARITY: Good. Few would deny that for today's reader, the NKJV is a great improvement in clarity over the 1611 original translation. The work could have gone considerably further in making changes to clarify and especially to give a smooth, contemporary English, but this would have resulted in losing more of its identity with the early King James Version. The results as they are remain good, a combination of the old and the new, but they reflect a desire to preserve rather than change, even though further clarification was possible.

From many examples of good changes, note the use of "Holy Spirit" instead of "Holy Ghost" at all times; see also such passages as 2 Corinthians 10:16b, "and not to boast in another man's line of things made ready to our hand," which has been made understandable in the NKJV, "and not to boast in another man's sphere of accomplishment."

Conclusion

Can one English translation of the Bible be recommended above all others? This final question cannot be answered by a simple "yes" or "no." It depends upon what a person wants most in the Bible he reads.

If he desires beautiful language, coupled with a respect for the past, with a ring of authenticity and **Reader Must** familiarity, the King James Version will be **Determine Goals** the selection. Its language is associated with the past, but this is not entirely against the King James. After all, Jesus lived in a certain time and place in the past. If one makes Jesus so contemporary that he cuts all ties to the past, this leaves Him as unhistorical. God did become flesh and lived among us in the person of His Son. The KJV conveys this fact to the heart of the reader or hearer. If one gets the feeling that this book has a quality different from other books, this, too, is in line with the truth. Although it is not literary quality that makes the difference, the dignity and depth of the King James Version is commensurate with the importance of God's communication with man. The New King James Version retains much of the

94

good qualities of the earlier version, and is recommended for today's generation in the place of the 1611 King James.

If one is approaching the Bible to study its words and concepts in a careful, comparative way, the New American Standard Bible is the best selection. This translation is accurate in form and detail. Using this translation with its **NASB Excellent for Study** helps and with a Bible concordance and a Bible dictionary, one can dig to new depths of understanding. Wherever he puts his shovel into its soil, he will unearth new treasures. But a translation cannot be both literal and natural at the same time. Although the NASB can be read with pleasure and understanding, the translation tends to become heavy with conscious adherence to the idioms of Hebrew or Greek.

The reader has still further needs. It is good to read a translation for the pure desire of receiving a fresh, clear message from God. There is the danger that one may archaize Jesus and leave Him bound to the first century. He really lived then, but He really lives now, too. The contemporary, readable language of the New International Version fills the need of making the Bible come alive for today's reader. With its high measure of accuracy and beauty, this translation contributes to the joy of reading God's Word in hours of meditation and discussion. Whether in the church or the home, whether for the Christian or the non-Christian, this version speaks in a vivid way.

The King James Version retains the beauty and majesty of the English language at its best, and the New King James adds more clarity and readability to its forebear. The New American Standard Bible presents an accurate, literal translation of Scripture, admirable for study in God's Word. The New International Version breathes with the freshness of God's living Word in a free-flowing expression—true and clear. Whether this combination or another, one needs to select with care translations of the Scripture, God's Word for people in every generation. Faithfulness is the keynote of translating God's Word—both in word and deed.

Books for Bible Study and Growth

The Lord of Promises, by LeRoy Lawson. Study the exciting promises of Jesus and learn the secret of an extraordinary life.
39989—$2.25 (Instructor 39988—$2.50)

The Bible Says, by Jack Cottrell. Find God's answers for contemporary ethical problems.
41014—$1.95

Selecting a Translation of the Bible, by Lewis A. Foster. Choose the English translation or translations that best suit your needs. Find what makes one translation "better" than another.
39975—$3.95

Available at your Christian bookstore or

STANDARD PUBLISHING